Puppet Magic

Joy L. Lowe and Kathryn I. Matthew

Neal-Schuman Publishers, Inc.
New York　　　　　　　　　　London

Published by Neal-Schuman Publishers, Inc.
100 William St., Suite 2004
New York, NY 10038

Printed and bound in the United States of America.

The paper used in this publication meets the minimum requirements of American National Standard for Information Sciences—Permanence of Paper for Printed Library Materials, ANSI Z39.48-1992.

ISBN-13: 978–1–55570–599–2

For Becky Callaway—KIM

*For my grandchildren: Skylar and Malachi Breczinski;
Katie, Trey, and Sara Lowe; and
Britt Thompson—JLL*

Contents

I. UP, UP WITH PUPPETS!

II. LEARN AND SHARE EASY PUPPET STORIES

III. THE PUPPET PATTERNS PANTRY

IV. PUPPET PLANET

List of Figures

Puppet Patterns

Foreword

"Read it again, Miz Salley!" "That's the bestest story, Miz Salley!" Those are some of the comments I heard over the nearly fifty years I've been involved in sharing literature with children. Almost my entire professional career was spent at the University of New Orleans as professor of children's literature. I am the author of several children's books and still go on school tours to share books with children.

Most children are eager and enthusiastic when it comes to hearing or seeing books and stories being shared with them. While many children are limited in their ability to read stories themselves, nearly all children love being read to or watching someone share literature with them in some other ways. There also are children who have difficulty with "trust" issues or lack confidence to interact with people.

And then—enter puppetry. Whether done by professionals or rank amateurs, puppetry is enjoyed by almost all children (and many adults). Puppetry seems "magical" to them and they do not mind "talking" to the puppets. Many teachers find this interaction valuable. The problem is that there are many more children than there are puppeteers.

Kathryn Matthew and Joy Lowe, two colleagues of mine, have collaborated to prepare this manual, designed for those with the desire to use puppets in sharing books, stories, and songs, but who lack the confidence or the "know-how" they think they must have to do so.

Matthew and Lowe describe how to select and purchase ready-made puppets, how to make puppets, and, perhaps most importantly, how to bring the puppets "to life" for their audiences (which can number from one to hundreds in size) and bring attitudes and expressions to use when sharing certain stories. They provide simple, step-by-step directions so that the readers can successfully give a simple puppet presentation.

The authors have been friends for many years. Dr. Lowe has had a multifaceted career as a librarian, classroom teacher, and college professor. She has three children (now grown and married) and six grandchildren on whom she has "practiced" her skills as a master storyteller and an amateur puppeteer. Her love of both children and children's literature is apparent throughout this book.

Dr. Matthew has been a classroom teacher and college professor for many years, and is an outstanding author of many books. I was introduced to her a long time ago when she became a student of mine and was the mother of two small boys (who she occasionally brought to class with her so that they could hear the stories). Those boys are now married and have careers of their own, but she tells me their love of literature remains.

Some years ago, I became acquainted with Dr. Lowe's puppet "presentations" (not "shows," she tells me) and was mesmerized. I wanted her to show me how to do them as well. She said I had to acquire some puppets first and then she would demonstrate how to manipulate them to tell a story. I never felt I could master that technique, so I remained a storyteller, perfecting my existing skills.

Puppet Magic reveals the secrets behind the tiny details that make a presentation successful. Reading it almost makes me want to try again! So readers, read the book, accept the challenge, and enjoy.

Professor Coleen C. Salley
Professional Storyteller

Preface

When puppets and stories come together, the effect can be magical. As the puppeteer weaves a tale, the puppets seem to come alive and captivate the audience. The performer fades into the background; the characters become the center of attention.

Storytelling with puppets is equally alluring whether the show uses an elaborate stage and expensive props or whether it consists of just a single character in the performer's lap. In *Puppet Magic,* we focus on the special appeal of one-person shows. While there are many books that explain how to create puppet theater presentations, few provide instructions for individual puppetry. For those who lack the space, money, or time needed for complicated productions, the techniques and materials presented in *Puppet Magic* will enable them to create their own simple and effective shows. Performances without a stage also allow the puppeteer to connect more directly with the viewers. Such shows can be carried out successfully with just a bit of rehearsal and a small audience in any setting that attracts children such as school libraries, public libraries, classrooms, and day care centers.

Puppet Magic is for librarians and others who are not sure how to begin as well as for readers with some experience who want to expand their skills. As we wrote *Puppet Magic*, we recorded and transcribed preparations and performances to ensure that we covered all the information and preparation necessary for an outstanding presentation.

Puppet Magic features complete scripts and instructions based on familiar nursery rhymes, fables, folktales, and picture books that thrill children yet require only a few characters. We also give step-by-step examples of how to adapt your own favorite stories. Techniques for deciding which stories to use, rehearsing, and voice projection are included. Practicing these techniques ensures that you will gain the skills and confidence you need to create unique characters and an engaging show.

In addition to purchasing information for ready-made puppets, we provide instructions for making handmade puppets. Such puppets can be one of the most appealing aspects of a show. After performances, children are often eager to create their own characters and tell stories using them. Young audience members can easily create many of the projects in *Puppet Magic*. The simple instructions use low-cost, easily obtainable materials and include full-size patterns and photographs. With these guidelines and a little imagination, an endless variety of puppets can be created.

BOOK ORGANIZATION

Puppet Magic divides the information necessary for a successful show into four parts: "Up, Up with Puppets!" "Learn and Share Easy Puppet Stories," "The Puppet Patterns Pantry," and "Puppet Planet."

Part I, "Up, Up with Puppets!" provides a primer to the world of puppetry. Chapter 1, "Introduction," includes a brief history of puppets and an overview of the various types of shows and puppets. Chapter 2, "Purchasing Puppets," offers advice on how to buy the right puppets for a particular need.

Chapter 3, "Easy Handmade Puppets," shows the reader how to make puppets using available materials. The characters in this detailed chapter are easy to make and versatile. Chapter 4, "It's Magic! Bringing Puppets to Life," explains a wide variety of performance issues, from how to prepare and select materials to rehearsal ideas, publicity, presentation techniques, and storage.

Part II, "Learn and Share Easy Puppet Stories," contains full scripts for a plethora of tales. Chapter 5, "Visiting Old Friends," explores programs based on nursery rhymes, fairy tales, and folktales. Chapter 6, "Meeting New Friends," guides readers in adapting popular picture books such as *The Very Hungry Caterpillar*, *Sylvester's Magic Pebble*, and *Peter Rabbit*. Each presentation offers suggested audience age levels, approximate length, characters and props, story annotations, suggested variations, and photographs.

Part III, "The Puppet Patterns Pantry," has patterns for creating all the characters described in Chapter 3 and many others. Photographs illustrate the complete project as well as each component part.

Part IV, "Puppet Planet," contains a wealth of resources, including sources for purchasing puppets and accessories, an extensive bibliography of additional titles and tools, a list of puppetry museums, and contact information for organizations that provide useful support including newsletters, grants, festivals, and online bulletin boards. This section also includes a chart listing the characters required to perform each of the stories in Part II.

Once you try a couple of the presentations, you'll discover that children of all ages respond to puppetry. Puppet shows can entertain, introduce books, and bring characters to life. By reading the chapters that follow and putting the ideas into practice, school librarians, public librarians, teachers, and parents will discover that combining stories and puppets not only delights children but also develops in them a love of books and reading.

I

UP, UP WITH PUPPETS!

1

INTRODUCTION

Have you ever sat in front of your television set mesmerized by the characters' actions, oblivious to the fact that you are watching puppets? Every day young television audiences learn from puppets as they are being entertained. Librarians and teachers with good stories and a few puppets can present puppet shows that have similar effects on audiences of all ages. Puppet shows can be performed in small spaces with limited funds, and they generate public enthusiasm for the library (Hunter, 1997).

Burr Tillstrom's *Kukla, Fran, and Ollie*, a puppet show for children, had a large adult audience when it appeared on television in the 1940s and 1950s. *The Howdy Doody Show* featured a marionette, Howdy Doody, along with real actors portraying Buffalo Bob Smith and Clarabelle Hornblower. Shari Lewis and sock puppet Lamb Chop taught children moral lessons. Puppets featured in *Mr. Rogers' Neighborhood* and on *Captain Kangaroo* taught children how to handle problems and how to get along with others. Jim Henson's Muppets, featured on *Sesame Street*, teach children skills to help them succeed in school and in life. The puppets on *Between the Lions* inhabit a magical library where book characters spring to life. Young viewers develop their reading skills and discover the joy of reading as they enjoy the antics of the lion family and their friends. This notable collection of marionettes, sock puppets, rod puppets, and hand puppets entrance audiences of all ages who suspend disbelief as they embrace these lively characters and accept them as real. *The Art of the Puppet* (Baird, 1965) has a wonderful chapter on the history of American puppetry, if you are interested in learning more.

Lots of puppets and an elaborate stage are not needed to entertain and teach. A single puppet in the hands of a librarian, a teacher, or a parent can entertain and teach a single child, a group of children, or an adult audience as puppet and puppeteer weave a magical tale (Hunter, 1997). Stories and puppets can be shared in settings ranging from public libraries and school libraries to classrooms, churches, and nursing homes. This book is for amateur and semiprofessional puppeteers who want to use puppets to share literature.

PUPPETS IN THE LIBRARY

"Can you tell me what cancer is?" a five-year-old boy asked a puppet perched on the hand of a librarian. Hesitant to ask an adult, this kindergarten student felt safe asking the puppet. The puppet shared a brief answer with the child and suggested that he share his question with his father. The librarian had just finished telling the kindergarten class a story about death in a dinosaur family. In the story a young dinosaur asked questions about death. Unbeknownst to the librarian, the boy had recently lost his mother to cancer and he was previously unwilling to talk about her death. While most children his age know that puppets cannot actually speak, they are more comfortable having a dialogue with an inanimate figure. Certainly this child was able to express his fear and lack of understanding more easily with a puppet than with a person.

Children especially enjoy hearing stories told to them by puppets. The puppets on *Sesame Street* and *Between the Lions* enter children's homes daily. Children are used to seeing them, they feel comfortable with them, and they recognize them as friends who share books and learning with them. Seeing a live puppet performance in the library reinforces these positive encounters with books and learning. After a puppet show in the library, children can check out the featured books and take them home to read again and again.

Puppet shows and storytelling programs encourage children to read and increase library circulation (Nespeca, 1990). Children enjoy listening to stories more than once whether the stories are read to them or told to them. Multiple exposures to the same book and opportunities to retell the story help develop children's literacy skills. Puppets add an exciting twist to retelling stories, and they help children develop language and literacy skills. Puppets encourage children to communicate and to participate (Church, 2001). When children retell stories with puppets, they build their comprehension skills, develop their vocabulary, explore their own creativity, and practice their communication skills (Abrams, 2005). Puppets bring imaginations to life as children retell the stories and write their own stories for the puppets to perform. Puppets enable children to creatively interact with their world as they learn and explore.

Figure 1-1   Deanna by Puppet Revelation. Used with permission.

Figure 1-2   Crazy Cow Puppet by Axtell Expressions. © 2007 used with permission.

The animated actions of puppets hold children's attention and appeal to their sense of wonder (Lowe and Matthew, 2003). Children listen intently with wide-eyed anticipation as stories unfold through the voice of the storyteller and the actions of the puppets. Using puppets in library programs increases toddlers' attention spans (Church, 2001). Library programs are important for very young children, as they help them develop listening skills and self-control as they become comfortable with adults other than their caregivers (Moore, 2003).

Lively children respond animatedly to puppets and quiet children find them empowering. Children willingly communicate with and through puppets because puppets are nonthreatening and easily controlled. Children treat puppets as confidants and reveal secrets or wishes to them. After one puppet performance, a very quiet, timid child approached Joy. She placed a puppet on the child's hand, and in a very soft voice the child began talking directly to the puppet. Puzzled that the puppet did not respond, the child asked Joy why the puppet was not talking. Once the child understood that she had to supply the puppet's voice, she began conversing with the puppet, providing both voices (Lowe and Matthew, 2003).

TYPES OF PUPPETS

Puppets come in all shapes and sizes and may be operated by one person or several people. Hand puppets, glove puppets, finger puppets, and Topsy Turvy dolls are a few of the most versatile types. Other puppeteers may prefer to use string, rod, and shadow puppets. We have included short descriptions of the different types of puppets you may want to consider for your presentations.

Hand Puppets

Hand puppets are the most frequently used type of puppet. They usually consist of just the head of the figure being portrayed. In puppets with moveable mouths, the puppeteer's hand fits over the top and bottom of the mouth. Large hand puppets have an opening for the arm of the puppeteer, whose hand goes all the way through the puppet to the mouth. The puppeteer appears to be almost wearing the puppet. Large, realistic hand puppets easily come to life before an audience and entrance audiences.

Full-body and half-body puppets are larger than traditional hand puppets and are more easily seen by larger audiences. Half-body puppets portray the character from the waist up, and full-body puppets portray the whole character and have legs that are usually detachable. Half-body and full-body puppets are usually people rather than animals or fantasy objects. They have hinged mouths, which are easy to

Figure 1-3   Girl Puppet by Playful Puppets. Used with permission.

manipulate. Some of them have arms and hands large enough for the puppeteer to insert his or her own arm and hand, which makes it easy for the puppeteer to hold and use props to help tell the story. Some of these puppets have metal rods for maneuvering the arms. The metal rods are about the size of the metal parts of coat hangers, are lightweight, and are easy to manipulate with practice.

Finger Puppets

Figure 1-4   Finger Puppets by Janis Nelson. Used with permission.

Finger puppets cover the fingertips. They can be used to enhance simple finger plays for small groups of preschool and kindergarten children. Tuck a finger puppet into your pocket and use it to instantly capture the attention of disruptive or bored youngsters. Finger puppets delight youngsters who are anxious to try them on their small fingers so they can perform their very own puppet shows. *Finger Folk: Reading Activities, PK-K* (Lohnes, 1999) has finger plays and patterns for creating finger puppets.

Another version of finger puppets is flat paper puppets with two holes in the torso for sticking your fingers through. While less suited to puppet shows, they are easy and inexpensive puppets that children can create to stage their own puppet shows or for story retelling. Students enjoy making small stages out of shoeboxes and cereal boxes.

Glove Puppets

Glove puppets may have a different character on each finger, or the fingers of the glove may be the legs of the puppet. Songs such as "Old MacDonald" and nursery rhymes including "Three Blind Mice" are well suited for telling with finger puppets and glove puppets. An Old MacDonald glove puppet will have the farmer on one finger and four different animals on the other fingers. As you sing the song you simply raise the appropriate finger so the audience can see the animal. For a bee or spider glove puppet your fingers are the legs, which makes the antics of these puppets fun to watch. Glove puppets, like finger puppets, are easy to pack and transport should you be called on to do puppet shows in different locations. They appeal to audiences both young and old and are best suited for puppet shows to small groups. Like finger puppets and hand puppets, glove puppets do not require a stage.

String Puppets

Figure 1-5   String Puppets by House of Puppets

String puppets or marionettes are jointed complete body puppets suspended from lightweight boards with as many as nine strings. The strings are attached to the puppet's head, shoulders, seat, hands, and knees. Manipulating the strings brings the puppets to life, which takes skill and constant practice to be successful. Present-day marionettes often have detachable strings, which can easily be untangled should they become tangled during a performance. It takes several puppeteers to put on shows with these puppets.

Rod Puppets

Rod puppets have a central rod anchored in their heads that is their basic support. Usually additional rods are suspended from the rod puppet's arms and feet to create more realistic movements. The puppeteer needs both hands available to operate these puppets. Practice and skill are required to effectively perform with rod puppets, but with practice and patience even children can perform with them. If more than one puppet is required for a performance, usually more than one puppeteer operates the puppets.

Shadow Puppets

Shadow puppets are flat-silhouetted figures with one or two rods that extend either below or behind the puppets. They are held up to a translucent screen that is lit from behind which casts a shadow over them. The audience on the other side of the screen views the antics of the animated shadows rather than the puppets themselves. These performances are more representational than realistic, which makes them more suitable for audiences of older children and adults.

Figure 1-6   Rod Puppet by M. S. Creations

Figure 1-7   Shadow Puppet

Topsy Turvy Dolls

While not puppets, these multicharacter dolls easily lend themselves to storytelling. For example, there is a Beauty and the Beast doll that has Beauty on one side and the Beast on the other side. When you turn the doll upside down and pull her skirt over her head, you find the Beast that becomes the Prince by turning the doll sideways. There is a similar one for telling the story of the Frog Prince. When you flip the Princess over and pull her skirt over her head, the Frog beneath becomes the Prince when you turn the doll sideways. Look for these unusual dolls in toy catalogs and exhibit booths at conventions. The North American Bear Company makes Topsy Turvy dolls, but it does not sell directly to the public. A quick Internet search will reveal not only outlets for purchasing the dolls but also patterns for making the dolls. When you are traveling to performances it is at times easier to take along one multicharacter doll than to carry several puppets. The dolls, just like puppets, make the stories come alive for children.

TYPES OF PUPPET SHOWS

Effective puppet shows may feature just the puppeteer and a few puppets corresponding to favorite children's books, nursery rhymes, songs, and folktales. The puppeteer can simply stand or sit in front of an audience and allow the puppets to tell their stories. Puppet shows without stages are ideal for traveling puppeteers who perform in "off-site" locations such as classrooms, community centers, or nursing homes, because a few puppets and props are easy to transport and nonstaged shows require less preparation time.

Should you decide to use a stage, remember that when you are hidden behind the stage you will not be able to see your audience. If your audience is children, you will need another adult sitting with the children as you perform. Puppet stages give the puppeteer the option of remaining hidden from view, which encourages reserved or reluctant puppeteers to perform (Jones, 2006).

Figure 1-8   Puppeteer and Puppets without a Stage

Figure 1-9   Sideways Table Puppet Stage

Sometimes a teacher or librarian will turn a table on its side and have the performance above the table's edge. Using a table for a puppet stage simply requires a square or rectangular table that can be turned on its side. (See Figure 1-9.) Glance around your library or your classroom for a table that can be cleared, turned on its side, and used for puppet performances. Unless the table is very wide you will need to sit on the floor to remain hidden from your audience. Place your puppets nearby in the order in which you will use them in your presentation. This quick, easily created stage is a favorite for children who want to create their own puppet shows using hand puppets, glove puppets, or stick puppets.

Figure 1-10   Doorway Puppet Stage

A curtain rod and a bed sheet can quickly transform a doorway into a puppet stage. (See Figure 1-10.) Pick an out-of-the-way door that has room for your audience in front and room for you and your puppets behind. Locate a spring-loaded curtain rod and adjust it to fit in the doorframe. Drape a bed sheet over the curtain rod. You will need a small chair to sit on as you manipulate the hand puppets over your head. Your head should be below the bed sheet. Should you be working with several puppets, have them on a table nearby so that you can easily switch between puppets. Hand puppets, glove puppets, and stick puppets work well with this type of theater.

Figure 1-11   Shadow Puppet Stage

A shadow puppet show requires a translucent screen with a light shining behind. (See Figure 1-11.) The puppet is placed against the screen and the shining light creates the shadow figure on the screen. Cutting the bottom out of a cardboard box and covering the opening with translucent paper is a quick and easy way to make a shadow puppet stage. Place a bright desk lamp behind the stage to cast a shadow on the puppets.

Collapsible, transportable stages can be made of lightweight materials. The portable puppet stage in Figure 1-12 was constructed of wood and fabric. Hinges allow it to fold down for storage and for transporting to different locations.

Figure 1-12   Portable Puppet Stage

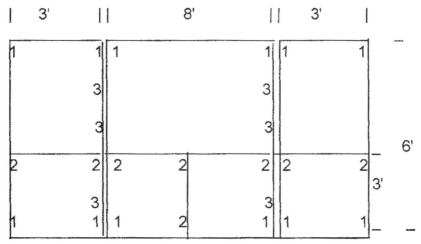

Figure 1-13   Portable Puppet Stage Diagram

Materials

Six 6-foot 1-inch by 2-inch pine boards

Three 8-foot 1-inch by 2-inch pine boards

Seven 3-foot 1-inch by 2-inch pine boards

Twelve 3-inch by 3-inch right-angle mending plates—Position 1

Eight 3-inch by 3-inch T mending plates—Position 2

Six 2-inch by 4-inch hinges—Position 3

Two hundred ¾-inch screws

Ten yards of solid-color fabric

Staples and staple gun

Directions

1. Lay out the lumber on a flat surface.
2. Square the corners.
3. Mount the right-angle mending plates in Position 1.
4. Mount the T mending plates in Position 2.
5. Mount the hinges in Position 3, spaced equally apart.
6. Stretch the fabric over the frame and staple it in place.

Puppet stages are as varied as the puppeteers who perform them and the puppets they use. Television shows such as *Sesame Street* have elaborate, permanent stages that accommodate a variety of puppets from life size to very small and allow for interactions with human actors. Vietnamese water puppetry has puppeteers standing in chest-high water performing behind curtain backdrops while the puppets perform on top of the water. Puppet stages do not have to be elaborate, and if you are interested in purchasing a puppet stage, several stores listed in Source A of the "Puppet Planet" in the back of the book sell puppet theaters. The puppetry books listed in Source D include instructions for constructing a wide variety of puppet stages (Carreiro, 2005; Crepeau and Richards, 2003; Henson and the Muppet Workshop, 1994; Latshaw, 2000; Minkel, 1999; Ross, 1969; Rottman, 1995).

The most magical aspect of puppetry is the effect puppet shows have on children. Puppet performances engage, entertain, and emotionally involve children as they willingly suspend disbelief and become wrapped up in the magic of puppets. The joy and excitement of live performances spark children's imaginations and introduce them to the pleasures of stories.

REFERENCES

Abrams, Pam. 2005. "The Pleasures of Puppets." *Scholastic Parent and Child* 78 (February/March): 66–68.

Baird, Bil. 1965. *The Art of the Puppet*. New York: MacMillan.

Carreiro, Carolyn. 2005. *Make Your Own Puppets and Puppet Theaters*. Nashville, TN: Williamson.

Church, Ellen Booth. 2001. "Using Puppets as Language-Building Partners." *Early Childhood Today* 16 (October).

Crepeau, Ingrid M., and M. Ann Richards. 2003. *A Show of Hands: Using Puppets with Young Children*. St. Paul, MN: Redleaf.

Henson, Cheryl, and the Muppet Workshop. 1994. *The Muppets Make Puppets*. New York: Workman.

Hunter, Lynn S. 1997. Piscataway's Puppet Program. In *School Library Journal's Best* ed. Lillian N. Gerhardt. New York: Neal-Schuman.

Jones, Elka. 2006. You're a What? Puppeteer. *Occupational Outlook Quarterly* 50 (Summer): 34–35.

Latshaw, George. 2000. *The Complete Book of Puppetry*. Mineola, NY: Dover Publications.

Lohnes, Marilyn. 1999. *Finger Folk: Reading Activities, PK-K*. Fort Atkinson, WI: Alleyside Press.

Lowe, Joy L., and Kathryn I. Matthew. 2003. Puppets and Prose: Using Puppets and Children's Literature in the Science Classroom. In *Mixing It Up: Integrated, Interdisciplinary, Intriguing Science in the Elementary Classroom* ed. Susan Koba. Arlington, VA: National Science Teachers Association Press.

Minkel, Walter. 1999. *How to Do "The Three Bears" with Two Hands: Performing with Puppets.* Chicago: American Library Association.

Moore, Kimberly B. 2003. Let's Go to the Library! *Scholastic Parent and Child* 10 (April/May): 59.

Nespeca, Sue McCleaf. 1990. Libraries Can Attach Illiteracy. *School Library Journal* 36 (July): 20–22.

Ross, Laura. 1969. *Hand Puppets: How to Make and Use Them.* Mineola, NY: Dover Publications.

Rottman, Fran. 1995. *Easy-to-Make Puppets and How to Use Them.* Ventura, CA: Gospel Light.

2

❦

PURCHASING PUPPETS

Searching for just the right puppets to purchase for your collection is an ongoing adventure. There are many puppets to choose from, such as realistic animals, fantasy creatures, people, and storybook characters. They come in a variety of shapes, sizes, colors, and styles. There are hand puppets, finger puppets, glove puppets, marionettes, rod puppets, and shadow puppets. When you are searching for puppets to use in a particular story, have a clear concept of exactly what you are looking for. Do you need a realistic puppet, a fantasy puppet, a serious puppet, or a comical puppet? Also keep in mind the size of the group you are presenting to, the size of the space you will be using, and the ages of the audience members. Large spaces and large audiences require large puppets that can easily be seen. In this chapter are ideas for building your puppet collection, a puppet purchasing checklist, and ideas for what to look for when you shop for hand puppets, finger puppets, and glove puppets.

Figure 2-1   Steve Axtell with Axtell Expressions Puppets. © 2007 used with permission.

BUILDING YOUR PUPPET COLLECTION

Toy stores, gift shops, mall kiosks, mail order catalogs, and online stores are all wonderful sources for puppets. Purchasing puppets in toy stores, gift shops, and mall kiosks provides you an opportunity to try them on for size. When you find just the right puppet for your collection in a mail order catalog or an online store, check the company's return policy in case the puppet does not fit your hand or cannot be easily manipulated. If you find just the puppet you need and it does not fit, however, you can use it as a prop as you tell the story.

Buy the highest quality puppets you can afford, as they will hold up through frequent use. Buying cheap puppets can end up being costly later, as they will not last. Once you begin telling stories you will find that the puppets are being used a great deal and high-quality puppets will withstand the wear and tear much better than less expensive ones. Spend more money on the puppets that you know you will use a great deal such as boys, girls, dogs, snakes, turtles, and rabbits. Folkmanis puppets are noted for their quality construction, their ability to withstand multiple performances, and their realistic appearances. (See Figure 2-2.) Pictures of Folkmanis puppets appear throughout this book. Axtell Expressions is another excellent source for puppets and props. (See Figure 2-1.) Information on these and other puppet sources can be found in Part V, "Puppet Planet." When you find suppliers that have puppets that appeal to you, keep a file with a notation of their names, addresses, and information about the puppets that you purchased.

Figure 2-2   Folkmanis Puppets. Used with permission.

Once you begin collecting puppets, you will find them staring at you from unexpected perches. When you sight a visually appealing puppet that is unique, you will find that you cannot resist adding it to your collection. Sometimes you will find a different version or style of a puppet you already own. For example, you might collect several different wolf puppets, from comic cartoon ones to realistic, lifelike ones. These various wolf puppets allow you to perform a variety of stories, fables, and poems, each with just the right wolf puppet to portray the different characters.

One way to build your collection is to look for puppets when you are traveling or on vacation. You might consider purchasing puppets when you travel as souvenirs of your trips. Puppets usually cost no more than other souvenirs might. Getting large puppets home on planes can be a problem; however, many stores will ship them home for you.

Building a puppet collection can be, but need not be, an expensive hobby. Familiar storybook characters have been transformed into puppets and are oftentimes packaged with copies of the books. Familiar tales and songs such as "The Three Billy Goats Gruff," "The Old Lady Who Swallowed a Fly," and "Old Macdonald Had a Farm" are packaged as sets that contain all of the puppets and props you need for your presentation. Purchasing a set gives you several puppets for a modest price, and many of the puppets can be used to tell multiple stories.

Start small and use homemade as well as purchased puppets. Do not be concerned that homemade puppets may not look as professional as purchased ones. Remember that the puppet is an idea, a suggestion that you are trying to share with the children. Children have wonderful imaginations, and even the simplest puppets come to life in their eyes.

PURCHASING PUPPETS CHECKLIST

When that very special puppet catches your eye and beckons, you will find yourself unable to resist removing it from its perch and slipping it over your hand. Take a few minutes to play with the puppet, using one of your favorite puppet voices. Then, if you think it is the puppet you have been looking for or one that you just have to have, take a minute to go through the hand puppet purchasing checklist in Figure 2-3 to make sure it is the puppet for you. Before you spend your money, you want to make sure that you are purchasing a puppet that you will be able to use over and over again.

	Does your hand fit comfortably inside the puppet?
	Is it too loose or too tight?
	Can you manipulate any moveable parts such as the head or arms?
	Is there a stiff seam or anything inside of the puppet poking your hand?
	Does the puppet feel soft or stiff?
	Is the stitching secure?
	Is there a stray thread that might cause a seam to unravel?

Figure 2-3   Hand Puppet Purchasing Checklist

1. Does your hand fit comfortably inside the puppet? Slip your hand inside the puppet and determine how it feels. The more comfortable the puppet feels on your hand, the more natural your movements will be. Fake fur, Antron Fleece, also known as Muppet Fleece, and fabric are some of the common materials used to make puppets, and each material feels different on your hand. Stretchy fabric has more give, making the puppets easier to manipulate. A stiff fake fur will have less give and the puppets may be difficult to manipulate.

2. Is it too loose or too tight? A puppet that is too loose is more likely to fall off when you make the puppet run or jump. A puppet that is too tight is difficult to remove during a presentation if you have to switch puppets as you tell the story. If you have a story in mind for the puppet, put the puppet on your hand and try out some of the movements you will use in your performance.

3. Can you manipulate any moveable parts such as the head or arms? Determine if the head and arms move easily by spending some time working them. Some puppets have a neck that moves independently from the rest of the body, which enables you to turn the head from side to side without turning the entire puppet. This feature is important when you are trying to make the puppet seem alive even when it is not speaking. If the puppet has a moveable mouth, open and close it to see if it moves easily. Check the mouth plate to make sure it is sturdy enough to withstand repeated use.

4. Is there a stiff seam or anything inside the puppet poking your hand? Make sure the seams are malleable enough to be comfortable and to allow you to easily manipulate the puppet. A puppet made of very stiff fabric may have stiff seams that hinder the movements of the puppet and scrape against your hand. There are frequently plastic hooks or ties attached to the puppet that can poke and scratch your hand if not removed.

5. Does the puppet feel soft or stiff? Manipulate the puppet and see if the softness or stiffness of the puppet hinders or helps your performance. Young audience members will be anxious to touch and hold your puppet, so you want it to be soft to the touch.

6. Is the stitching secure? This is very important, as nothing is more frustrating to both the puppeteer and the audience than accidents that happen because of a poorly constructed puppet. After repeated use, seams may separate, causing small holes that will reveal your hand.

7. Is there a stray thread that might cause a seam to unravel? Check to see if the thread can be tied off or if it can be clipped.

HAND PUPPETS

When a hand puppet perched on a shelf beckons you, take it down and try it on to see if it fits comfortably on your hand. Manipulate any moveable parts such as the head, hands, and mouth. Look for puppets with moveable mouths that you can open and close as the puppets speak. Puppets with moveable mouths seem more real to your audience. The more comfortable the puppet is on your hand, the more natural you will be able to make its movements. A puppet that is too loose may fall off your hand during a performance, and a puppet that is too tight will constrict your movements. Some hand puppets are soft and flexible, and others are stiff and less supple, so you will want to try them on and see how easy or difficult they are to manipulate. If the character you are portraying is very active, then you probably want a soft, flexible puppet. Poorly constructed puppets or those with loose threads are likely to come apart during a performance, which will frustrate both the audience and the puppeteer, so carefully check the construction of the puppet before you buy it.

FINGER PUPPETS

Finger puppets are made to fit on your individual fingers, so each finger can hold a different character. These tiny gems start with a tube that slips over your finger. The tiny tube can be transformed into an amazing variety of characters including animals, bugs, people, storybook characters, and fantasy creatures. From circus animals to community helpers to special holiday characters, the variety of finger puppet sets is extensive. Purchasing a set of finger puppets gives you an entire cast of characters for a modest price. Consider purchasing a set of finger puppets to accompany "The Old Lady Who Swallowed a Fly," which includes a fly, a spider, a bird, a cat, a dog, a goat, a cow, and a horse. This same set of finger puppets can be used for "Old MacDonald Had a Farm" and nursery rhymes including "The Itsy Bitsy Spider,"

"Pussycat, Pussycat," and "Hickory, Dickory Dock." Finger puppets are made from felt or crocheted from yarn. The crocheted finger puppets are the most flexible and stretch to fit over fingers of different sizes.

GLOVE PUPPETS

Glove puppets slip over your hand just like your winter gloves. Some glove puppets have a different character on each finger. When you consider purchasing this type of glove puppet, check to make sure that the glove is supple enough to let you easily move each finger up and down independently. For example, an Old MacDonald glove puppet would have the farmer on one finger and different animals on each of the other fingers. You would want to be able to hold up each finger individually as you and your audience sing about that animal. So wiggle your fingers around inside the glove and make sure it has a comfortable feel and fit.

Other glove puppets you might consider purchasing are designed so that the fingers of the glove are the legs of the animal. For example, the main part of the glove might be a turtle's shell and the fingers of the glove would be the legs of the turtle. To make the turtle creep, you will want to ensure that the glove allows you a good range of movement. Slip your hand into the glove, move your fingers, and walk the animal up your arm or across the store counter. Check to be sure that the seams of the glove are tightly sewn so that they will withstand frequent use.

Summary

When you discover wonderful new books for your library, you will find yourself mentally scanning your puppet collection to determine if you have the puppets you need to share the books with your audiences. If you do not have just the right puppets, you will find yourself searching for them. If you have difficulty finding just the right puppets, keep looking, because eventually you will find them, often in unlikely places. When word spreads of your interest in puppets, you will find that friends, relatives, and colleagues are bestowing puppets on you to add to your collection. As your collection grows, you will need to find ways to store your growing collection. Many of the puppet suppliers noted in Part V, "Puppet Planet," sell different ways to store puppets such as bins, poles, and hammocks.

3

EASY HANDMADE PUPPETS

Discover the magic in making your very own puppets and in sharing the magic with children. Following the simple directions in this chapter, you can quickly and cheaply craft felt puppets, paper plate puppets, sock puppets, and stick puppets. Some of the puppets are easy enough for children to make so they too can share in the magic of storytelling with puppets. Included are ideas for selecting and organizing your puppet-making supplies. Most of the patterns in Part III, "The Puppet Patterns Pantry," are full-size patterns. Accompanying the individual nursery rhymes, folktales, poems, and stories are the instructions for specific puppets.

SELECTING MATERIALS

Puppet-Making Basics

Start with a large, flat, well-lit surface for your puppet-making workspace, either a large table or a countertop with an electrical outlet nearby, enough room to spread out your patterns and materials, and room to assemble the puppets. Because you will probably be interrupted while working on the puppets, you will want to find a place where you can leave the materials unattended. A hot glue gun enables you to quickly assemble the puppets, but having a hot glue gun does mean your workspace needs to be inaccessible to small children.

Your local craft stores and fabric stores are excellent sources for purchasing the supplies you will need. If you are not familiar with all the wonderful items in these stores, spend time wandering up and down the aisles discovering their treasures and gathering ideas for your puppets. Take a minute to read the labels on the glue bottles and glue sticks to find out which ones are best for the different materials you will be using. Examine the wiggle eyes and pompoms, as they come in an assortment of sizes. Purchase packs of assorted sizes so that you have a variety to choose from as you begin crafting puppets. Examine all the colorful varieties of yarn and pick one or two for creating the hair on your puppets. Yarn comes in an interesting variety of textures and colors, each providing a different style of hair. Note the different colors of felt that are available and which store has the largest variety of colors. Look for small hats and other doll accessories that you can use for your puppets. Imagine how you can decorate your puppets using short lengths of ribbon and lace, small flowers, colorful buttons, and decorative beads. As you peruse the aisles and make your selections, set your imagination free to design and create one-of-a-kind puppets.

PUPPET-MAKING TOOLKIT

General materials used for making the puppets in this book include felt, socks, paper plates, craft sticks, a hot glue gun, glue, needles, thread, yarn, wiggle eyes, pompoms, chenille sticks, thin cardboard, scissors, a stapler, pencils, markers, and a ruler. Paper towel tubes, gloves, paper cups, markers, crayons, pipe cleaners, fake fur, ribbons, lace, oven mitts, fabric scraps, straws, beads, craft sticks, sequins, Styrofoam, ping-pong balls, cardboard, and packing peanuts can be used to transform felt, socks, and paper plates into unique puppets. Additional ideas for materials to use for creating puppets can be found in the books listed in Part IV at the end of the book. A sectioned tote tray with a handle is one way to store and organize your smaller craft tools such as wiggle eyes, pompoms, scissors, a stapler, needles, and thread. Copy paper boxes with lift-off tops are a convenient, easy way to store your materials from one puppet-making session to the next, or you may want to buy a plastic bin with a lid.

1. Felt

   Craft stores sell felt in 9-inch by 12-inch pieces that are just the right size for creating felt

Figure 3-1   Puppet-Making Toolkit

hand puppets. However, craft felt is thin and you may find that your puppets are more durable if you buy felt by the yard at a fabric store. Buy felt in an assortment of colors such as brown, black, white, red, blue, yellow, and pink. Save your felt scraps to make facial features and accessories for your puppets. Small oblong scraps or triangular scraps are perfect for eyes, noses, ears, and mouths. Think about using small white felt ovals topped with a small colored felt circle to create eyes or top the small white ovals with small wiggle eyes. A red rounded felt tongue can be tucked inside the mouth of a dog sock puppet and a forked felt tongue can dangle from the mouth of a snake sock puppet to add just the right finishing touch.

2. Socks

   Purchase a package of white men's tube socks from a discount store and transform them into an assortment of puppets. Or select some colorful, patterned women's socks to give your puppets distinctive looks.

3. Paper plates

   Buy the cheapest white paper plates you can find. These flimsy plates may not withstand the food at your picnic, but they are sturdy enough for hand puppets. Consider involving your young audiences in creating puppets from this affordable material.

4. Craft sticks

   Purchase a big bag of craft sticks for making stick puppets. Craft sticks are bigger and easier to work with than Popsicle sticks. Stick puppets are easy and cheap to make, so consider making a set for the members of your audience or providing them with the materials to make their own.

5. Hot glue gun

   Essential components of your puppet-making toolkit are a hot glue gun and glue sticks. The glue quickly and easily bonds your materials. Use caution, as the glue is very hot and dries quickly.

6. Glue

Read the labels on the bottles of glue to determine which ones you will need. The right glue for you depends on the materials you are using. You may want to start with an all-purpose craft glue such as Aleene's Original Tacky Glue.

7. Needle and thread

If you are handy with a needle and thread or a sewing machine, you may prefer to sew the felt puppets together rather than gluing them together. The patterns in this book include a ¼-inch seam allowance. Sew on the sock puppets' features, as the glue tends to soak through the socks.

8. Embroidery thread

Six strands of black or brown embroidery thread are just the right thickness for whiskers for cats, mice, and lions.

9. Yarn

Yarn is the perfect choice for hair on sock puppets. It does not take much yarn to make puppet hair, so if you have leftover bits of yarn, add them to your toolkit. Yarn comes in so many textures and so many colors it is hard to decide which yarn to buy. Think about your puppet's personality. If your puppet is serious or cautious, then select brown, black, or yellow yarn for its hair. For a playful or adventurous puppet, select blue, green, or purple yarn.

10. Chenille sticks

These fat, fuzzy sticks make bunny and cat whiskers and caterpillar and butterfly antennae. Buy a package of assorted colors so you will have lots of choices as you create your puppets. Use a sharp pair of scissors to trim the chenille sticks to just the right size.

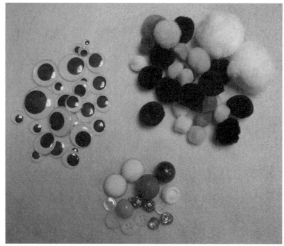

11. Pompoms

Select a bag of pompoms in assorted sizes and colors. Use them for eyes, noses, and buttons. Let the size of the puppet and the puppet's personality dictate the size and the color to use.

Figure 3-2   Wiggle Eyes, Pompoms, and Buttons

12. Wiggle eyes

Oval wiggle eyes in a variety of sizes are a must. Position them on the puppets' faces at different angles to create interesting facial expressions. Use large round wiggle eyes on frog sock puppets or on paper plate puppets. As you manipulate the puppets, their wiggle eyes help bring them to life.

13. Buttons

Collect small buttons in a variety of designs and colors. Use them to decorate the puppet's clothing, for eyes, or for noses.

14. Thin cardboard

The cardboard from twelve-packs of soft drinks and from cereal boxes is just the right thickness for lining the mouths of your sock puppets and for making puppet crowns and other accessories.

15. Scissors

    Use an all-purpose pair of scissors for cutting patterns, paper, thin cardboard, and yarn. You may want to have a separate pair of very sharp scissors that you use just for cutting fabric and felt.

16. Stapler and staples

    These essential tools allow you to quickly and easily put together paper plate puppets.

17. Pencils and markers

    Use pencils to trace the patterns and mark the locations for facial features. Use markers to add features or shadings to the puppets.

Tricks of the Trade

1. Hot glue gun

    A one- to two-foot length of wax paper makes an ideal working surface for using a hot glue gun. A great place to rest the hot glue gun is on a piece of ceramic tile; perhaps you have a piece of tile left over from a bathroom-remodeling project. Hot glue sets very quickly, so work on small sections at a time. When you are finished, allow the gun to cool completely before you store it. Burns from a hot glue are very painful, so be extremely careful and keep a bowl of ice water nearby to immerse burned fingers.

2. Sock puppets

    When adding features to sock puppets, position the sock on your hand with the heel facing up and use the heel for the top of the puppet's head. The heel is a good place to anchor the eyes because the heel has extra fabric to work with.

3. Eyes

    As you create the puppets, try out different kinds of eyes and different positions until you have just the look you want. Buttons, pompoms, small Styrofoam balls, the bowls of plastic spoons, and ping-pong balls can all be used for puppet eyes.

4. Mouths and tongues

    Experiment with different shapes and colors of felt for the mouths of felt hand puppets and the tongues of sock puppets. It takes only small scraps of felt for the mouths and tongues, so use whatever scraps you have on hand and try out different looks for your puppets.

MAKING PUPPETS

Imagine the Finished Product

Examining the photographs of the finished puppets before you begin will give you an idea of what your puppets will look like. As you create your puppets, keep in mind the characters' personalities and let their personalities guide you as you apply the finishing touches to their features.

Gather the Materials

Just as you check your pantry for all the ingredients in a recipe before you begin cooking, check you puppet toolkit to make sure you have all the materials you will need before you begin creating puppets. Check the list of materials needed in each of the following sections for creating basic felt hand puppets, sock puppets, paper plate puppets, and stick puppets. In each chapter there are lists of materials specific to the creation of the puppets used in the presentation, and the patterns for the puppets are found in the "Puppet Patterns Pantry" starting on page 129.

Follow the Directions

Step-by-step directions with accompanying photographs lead you through making the puppets. Generally, it is easier to add features such as eyes, mouth, and nose after the puppet base is assembled. Rummage through your puppet toolkit to find special touches to personalize each puppet. Try out different eyes, for example, wiggle eyes or felt circles or buttons. Does a pompom or a button work better for the nose? Should the hair be brown or yellow or blue? Let your imagination guide you.

Patterns

In the "Puppet Patterns Pantry" starting on page 129 most of the patterns are full-size and the easiest way to make copies of them is on a photocopier. Another option is to trace them by laying a thin sheet of paper over the patterns and tracing over them with a pencil. Any patterns that are not full-size have a notation on the page with the percent increase you need to put into the photocopier to create full-size patterns. The stick puppets patterns are all full-size. Make photocopies of these patterns on the heaviest paper your copy machine will allow.

FELT HAND PUPPETS

Tips

With the basic hand puppet patterns found on page 129, you can create people and animal puppets used throughout the book. This hand puppet fits comfortably on most adults' hands, and it can be made using two standard 9-inch by 12-inch pieces of felt. You may find it easier to cut out one piece at a time rather than stacking two pieces of felt together and cutting them both out at the same time. An assortment of items including felt scraps, wiggle eyes, buttons, lace, ribbon, fabric scraps, pompoms, and chenille sticks enable you to create a variety of puppets. By adding hair, hats, different eyes, and ears you can vary the look of the puppets to give each puppet its own distinct personality.

Finished Puppet

Materials

Two pieces of 9-inch by 12-inch felt for the body

Scraps of pink or brown felt for the face and hands

Scraps of white, pink, red, blue, or black felt for the eyes and mouth

Wiggle eyes (optional)

Craft glue

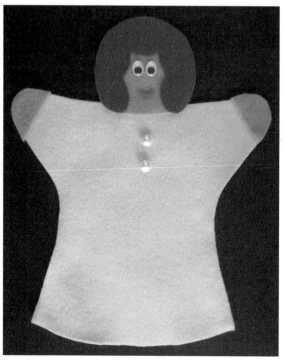

Figure 3-3　Basic Felt Hand Puppet

Hot glue and gun

Scissors

Directions

1. Photocopy or trace the patterns for the basic felt hand puppet, the hands, the face, the hair, the eyes, and the mouth. These patterns are in the "Puppet Patterns Pantry" starting on page 129. Cut out the patterns.
2. Cut two bodies from the basic hand puppet pattern using two 9-inch by 12-inch pieces of felt.
3. Cut out the hands and the face from the pink or brown felt scraps.
4. Glue the hands and face on the front body piece as shown in Figure 3-4.
5. Cut the hair from brown or yellow felt.
6. Glue the hair on the front of the face. (See Figure 3-3.)
7. Glue on small oval wiggle eyes or create the eyes from felt scraps. The patterns for the felt eyes are in the "Puppet Patterns Pantry" on page 130.
8. Create the eyes from white felt scraps by cutting two small ovals.
9. Glue the ovals on the face.
10. Cut two small circles from blue felt for the irises of the eyes.
11. Glue the irises on top of the ovals.
12. Cut the mouth from pink or red felt.
13. Glue the mouth on the face.
14. Sew two buttons on the center front of the dress, aligning them with the mouth. (See Figure 3-3.)
15. Glue or sew the front piece of the puppet to the back piece, leaving the bottom open to insert your hand.

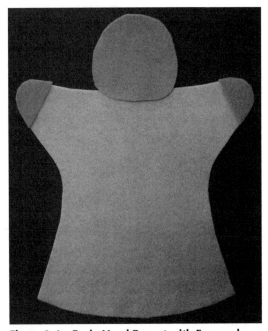

Figure 3-4   Basic Hand Puppet with Face and Hands

Figure 3-5   Basic Hand Puppet with Felt Eyes

PAPER PLATE PUPPETS

Tips

Transform thin white paper plates into a variety of puppets using paint, wiggle eyes, pompoms, chenille sticks, pipe cleaners, felt, buttons, glue, and scissors. Attach small features such as the eyes, noses, and mouths with craft glue. Attach the arms, legs, and whiskers with a hot glue gun. Fasten the paper plates together using either hot glue or a stapler. Using a hot glue gun around children can be dangerous, so if the children are creating paper plate puppets, have them use craft glue to attach the features and then staple the plates together for them. While these hand puppets do not have moveable features, they do hold the children's attention as you tell the story. When the puppet is speaking, move your hand from side to side so that the puppet appears to be making eye contact with your audience. When the puppet is not speaking, just hold it still. Paper plate puppets are simple enough for children to make with some assistance from you.

Finished Puppet

Figure 3-6   Cat Paper Plate Puppet

Materials

Three white paper plates

Two sheets white construction paper or photocopy paper

Three chenille sticks

Two large wiggle eyes

One pompom for nose

Small scrap of pink felt

Glue and glue gun

Stapler and staples

Scissors

Pencil

Directions

1. Photocopy or trace the patterns for the ears, the paws, and the tongue. These patterns are in the "Puppet Patterns Pantry" on page 131. Cut out the patterns.
2. Make two ears by placing the ear pattern on the bottom of one of the paper plates and trace around it.
3. Cut the ears out.
4. Cut three-fourths of the rim of the paper plate off to use as the tail.
5. Set the ears and the tail aside.
6. For the legs, take one of the pieces of white paper and fold it in fourths lengthwise. Cut the paper into four pieces.
7. Accordion-fold each piece of paper by folding the strips back over themselves an inch at a time. (See Figure 3-8.)

Figure 3-7   Ears and Tail

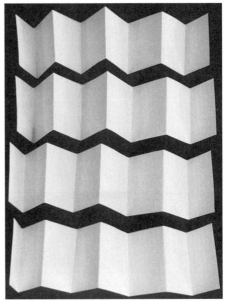

Figure 3-8   Accordion-Folded Strips of Paper

8. Place the paw pattern on a sheet of white paper and trace around it four times.
9. Cut out the paws.
10. Glue the paws to the ends of the legs. Set aside to let the glue dry.

Figure 3-9 Legs and Paws

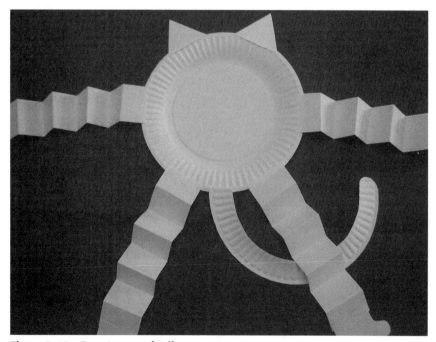

Figure 3-10 Ears, Legs, and Tail

11. Glue the ears, the legs, and the tail around the edges of one of the paper plates. Use Figure 3-10 as a guide for placing the pieces.
12. Set the puppet aside to let the glue dry.
13. With the hot glue gun, squirt a ribbon of glue around the edge of the paper plate. Leave an opening at the bottom between the legs just large enough to slip your hand inside.

Figure 3-11   Eyes and Whiskers

14. Use the photograph of the finished puppet in Figure 3-6 as a guide for gluing on the features.
15. Glue the wiggle eyes in the top third of the paper plate.
16. Glue the chenille stick whiskers in the center of the paper plate.
17. Glue the pompom on top of the whiskers right in the center.
18. Cut the tongue out of the scrap of pink felt.
19. Glue the tongue just below the pompom.
20. Set the puppet aside to let the glue dry.

SOCK PUPPETS

Tips

Transform white tube socks or colorful striped socks into fanciful puppets. For example, green socks are great for frog puppets and striped socks are just right for caterpillars. Buttons, pompoms, wiggle eyes, yarn, felt, ribbons, thin cardboard, glue, and scissors are the magic ingredients for converting socks into puppets. Slip your hand inside the sock, then try out different materials for the eyes, ears, and other features and determine the best placement for them. Use either craft glue or a needle and thread to attach the features to the socks. If you use hot glue, use only a small amount or it will seep right through the sock and onto your hand. Your hand movements will enable you to manipulate the puppet's face to change its expression.

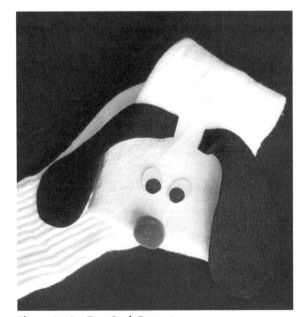

Figure 3-12   Dog Sock Puppet

Finished Puppet

Materials

Sock

Small pieces of black felt for the ears

Two wiggle eyes

One pompom for nose

Thin cardboard for forming the mouth

Pencil

Scissors

Glue

Ruler

Directions

1. Cut a circle from the thin cardboard. The circle should be about as wide as the sock. An easy way to do this is to find a glass that is as wide as the sock and trace around it. (See Figure 3-13.)
2. Bend the circle in half.
3. Turn the sock inside out.
4. Glue the bent circle of cardboard over the toe of the sock. Hold the cardboard in place for a few seconds and then set the sock aside for the glue to dry.
5. Turn the sock right side out.
6. Glue the wiggle eyes on 1 inch up from the edge of the mouth. (See Figure 3-14.)
7. Glue the pompom on the nose at the edge of the mouth just below the eyes.
8. Photocopy or trace the pattern for the ears. This pattern is in the "Puppet Patterns Pantry" on page 132. Cut out the patterns.
9. Cut two ears out of black felt.
10. Glue the ears on 2½ inches up from the edge of the mouth.
11. Set the puppet aside to let the glue dry.

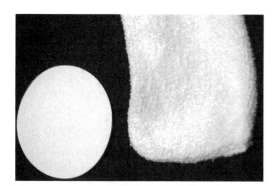

Figure 3-13   Cardboard Circle and Sock

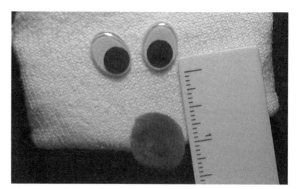

Figure 3-14   Eyes and Nose

STICK PUPPETS

Tips

Using paper or felt, craft sticks, glue, markers, crayons, and scissors, you can quickly and cheaply create stick puppets. These puppets are simple enough for children to make. Children can use the puppets to retell a story, or they can design and create their own puppets to perform their own stories.

Finished Puppet

Materials

Heavy paper

One craft stick

Glue

Markers

Scissors

Directions

1. Make photocopies of the goat pattern on heavy paper. This pattern is in the "Puppet Patterns Pantry" on page 133.
2. Use markers or crayons to color the puppet or leave the puppet white.
3. Cut the puppet out.
4. Glue the puppet to a craft stick.
5. Set the puppet aside to let the glue dry.

Figure 3-15   Goat Stick Puppet

4

IT'S MAGIC! BRINGING PUPPETS TO LIFE

Now that you have ideas for making and purchasing puppets, it is time to discuss how to present a puppet show. This chapter shows you how to select and prepare your material, provide publicity, manipulate puppets, rehearse your presentation, make your presentation, and store your materials. The key is to start with a simple, short presentation requiring only one puppet. As you build your skills and discover how much the children enjoy your presentations, you will be ready to work on longer presentations with two or more puppets and props. Once you get hooked on puppets and your audiences get hooked on puppets, you will wonder how you ever read or told stories without them.

SELECTING AND PREPARING MATERIAL

Think about nursery rhymes, short poems, or picture storybooks that you currently share with children. These favorite, familiar pieces will be easy for you to remember as you focus on adding a hand puppet to your storytelling. For example, you might select a nursery rhyme that has one main character that the audience can easily identify, such as "Jack, Be Nimble." With a boy puppet and a candlestick prop you are ready to begin. Nursery rhymes and songs are short and action packed and easily lend themselves to being told by a narrator, which means the storyteller does not have to use a variety of voices and can simply manipulate the puppets and props while reciting the rhyme or song. Audience members are often familiar with the nursery rhymes and songs, so they are eager to join in to say the words with you.

Should you stumble when presenting a nursery rhyme, chances are your audience will immediately correct you and take great delight in helping you. The rhyme and rhythm make it easy for children to join in as you recite the nursery rhymes. Encourage the children to join in as you repeat the rhymes by making eye contact with them, nodding your head, or signaling with simple hand gestures. Poems should be memorized because the poet has spent a great deal of time selecting just the right words and poems lose effectiveness if they are not presented as written by the poet. If you make a mistake, do not stop and correct yourself. Just keep going, and chances are your audience will not have noticed your mistake.

To memorize a poem, read it out loud several times. You may want to tape record your reading so that you can listen to the tape to help you with the memorization. After you read the poem out loud several times, cover all but the first line with your hand or a sheet of paper. Read the first line out loud one more time, cover the line, and recite it. Check to see if you recited it correctly. If you did not, read it out loud several more times, then cover it, and recite it. Once you have the first line memorized, read the first two lines out loud several times. Cover the lines and try to recite them. Each time you memorize another line, uncover the next line and repeat the procedure until you have memorized the entire poem. You can tape record yourself reciting the poem and then play the tape back as you look at the poem. Underline any words or phrases that you need to spend more time memorizing. If you have a willing colleague, have that person look at the poem as you recite it and correct you if you make any mistakes or simply underline any mistakes you make. Some people find that writing the poem as they say it out loud helps them memorize. Experiment to determine which method works best for you.

Once you have mastered presenting nursery rhymes and poems with puppets, you are ready to present stories. As you browse through your favorite picture storybooks, look for stories with simple plots, one or two main characters, one or two scenes, action, and conflict. Think about cumulative tales or those with repeating refrains. In cumulative tales, the events build on each other, which makes the story easier to remember. "The Old Lady Who Swallowed a Fly" is an example of a cumulative tale, and there are several different storybook versions available on which to base your presentation. Stories with repeated refrains are easy to memorize and encourage audience participation, as the children can join you each time you repeat the refrain. Encouraging the audience to participate actively involves them in the presentation, which holds their attention and makes the presentation more fun for them and for you.

Folktales and fairy tales are action-packed, condensed stories that are short and dramatic. They have a well-defined beginning, middle, and end. The problem is quickly introduced at the beginning of the story, the middle of the story consists of attempts to solve the problem, and the tale usually comes to a satisfying conclusion in which the problem is solved. Folktales and fairy tales often have magical elements that add to the suspense and excitement of the story. They are short and easy to adapt to puppet presentations, as they are filled with action and dialogue. The action and the dialogue hold the audience's interest and allow for dramatic interpretations by you and your puppets. Locate different versions of the folktales and fairy tales, read through them all, and select the one that you like or combine elements from different versions to create your own version.

Begin preparing for your presentation by reading the story several times until you become familiar with it. You may find it helpful to create a visual map of the story or an outline of the story to help you remember the sequence of events. In the map or outline, include the key events in the story so that you retain the story structure. Print out your map or outline in a fourteen-point font or larger and double spaced so you can read it easily as you perform. When you first tell the story, you may find it helpful to have the visual map or the outline nearby. If you stand behind a podium for your presentation, you can place the visual map or the outline on the podium so that you can easily glance at it as you present. If you are seated, place a table beside you to hold your notes, books, and puppets.

Whereas it is important to memorize a rhyme or poem, it is not necessary to memorize a story or a script. Memorized stories lack spontaneity and freshness and result in presentations that are stiff and unnatural. You want your performance to be relaxed and natural, so it is better if you just tell the story in your own words. This also allows you to inject your own personality into the story, to embellish the story, and to create your own interpretation. You probably do not want to change chants or repeated refrains that your audience will expect to hear such as "Poor old lady, she'll probably die" from "The Old Lady Who Swallowed a Fly" or "E-I-E-I-O" from "Old MacDonald Had a Farm."

When you select material for your presentation, start by thinking about your audience's age range, how many audience members you anticipate, the size of the room, and how much time you will spend performing. If the audience is very young, you will want to select very short, simple presentations; for older audiences, you will want to select longer pieces. For very young children with short attention spans, use nursery rhymes or short poems with accompanying sounds and actions. Young children enjoy hearing the rhymes and poems more than once and want to participate in the action. To keep early elementary students engaged, present a diverse collection of stories and poems. Students in upper elementary grades have longer attention spans and are able to sit through longer presentations. They also enjoy presentations that include a variety of stories and poems. Students of all ages enjoy being actively involved in the presentations and are eager to participate.

COPYRIGHT AND PERMISSIONS

Adapting and performing copyrighted material in libraries and schools requires permission from the publisher, as these are considered public performances (Minkel, 2000). Folktales, nursery rhymes, and songs that are in the public domain can be adapted without permission. If you use the exact words or reproduce characters from illustrations of a copyrighted edition of a folktale, nursery rhyme, or song, however, you will need permission from the publisher to use this in your performance. In order to obtain permission to use the material, you should contact the permissions department of the publisher. This may take several weeks and may involve a fee. Requests for permissions need to be in writing through email, fax, or the postal service. The request should include your name, your contact information, the title of the work, the name of the author and/or illustrator, the ISBN, a brief description of your intended audience, whether or not fees will be charged for the presentation, and a brief description of how you plan to adapt and use the poem, story, or song. Requests sent through the mail should include a stamped self-addressed envelope for the publisher to mail the response. Many publishers have permission forms on their Web sites.

PUBLICITY

Once you have decided on the material you will present and have obtained permission to present the material, you are ready to publicize your performance. Decide on a date, time, location, audience ages, and approximate length of the program, which should be determined by the ages of the audience members. Decide on the best way to publicize the program. It may be a simple flyer that is posted in the library, or it might be press releases that are sent to a radio station or a newspaper. The information should include who, what, where, when, and why.

If you are presenting a puppet show in your school library, you can advertise by placing flyers in teachers' mailboxes, posting them on school bulletin boards, or sending them home to parents in students' backpacks. Be sure the flyers include the date, the time, the location, your name, your contact information, and a brief blurb about the content of the program. Prior to the event when classes come to the library, talk to the students about the puppet show or give them a brief preview.

Puppet shows in public libraries take more coordinating, planning, and publicizing. The date, time, and room may need to be coordinated with other activities in the library. Flyers posted in the library and available for patrons to take home are one way to advertise the program. Library staff members can mention the puppet show to patrons as they check out books. Flyers can also be sent to local schools and organizations. Sending press releases to the local newspapers, radio stations, and television stations are excellent ways to advertise your program to a wide audience. Find out the name of the person you can send the press releases to and develop a personal relationship with that person. One librarian admits to baking brownies and taking them to her local newspaper office along with her press releases.

Start the press release with your name and contact information. Directly below, centered on the page in all caps, type a catchy, strong headline to grab the readers' attention. Then type in a subhead that gives more details in order to hook the readers. For example,

STORIES COME TO LIFE
Master Storyteller Joy Lowe Entrances Audiences with Puppets and Stories

Follow the subhead with a lead paragraph that tells who, what, when, where, and how. Be sure to include everything the reader needs to know in this lead paragraph. Keep the paragraph succinct. The remaining one or two paragraphs should include details that support what you wrote in the lead paragraph. Consider putting in a quote from an excited audience member from a previous presentation. Send the press releases out several weeks before the performance.

MANIPULATING PUPPETS

Puppets provide a visual focus to your storytelling and reinforce the story events, which help children remember the story. It is important to keep the puppet visible to everyone in the audience and to keep it moving and active. The puppet's movements should be realistic and purposeful, to make it look as though it is alive. The movements do need to be purposeful rather than just bobbing around or swaying back and forth. Hold the puppet in a natural position. For example, a cat may be held in the crook of your arm or a snake draped over your arm. As you speak, move the puppet's arms and head to attract the audience's attention and to show emotion. One way to show emotion is to tilt the puppet's head. For example, if the puppet is sad or shy, it might be looking down. Hand puppets' movements can include jumping, walking, clapping, sneezing, waving, bending, turning, bowing, picking up objects, and dropping objects. Practicing will ensure that the puppet's movements are smooth and natural. To make the movements more noticeable or to add humor to the presentation, you can exaggerate them. Exaggerated, slow, deliberate movements are easier for the audience to see. Moving the puppet's arms and mouth at the same time takes practice. As you practice manipulating puppets, you will develop the muscles in your hands, and this will give your puppet's movements more effect. Oversized props are easier to manipulate in the puppet's tiny hands, and they are also easier for the audience to see.

The puppet should make eye contact with the audience unless it is speaking directly to you. By bending your hand downward, you can make the puppet's eyes focus on the audience members' eyes. You want the puppet's eyes to make direct contact with the audience members' eyes. Slowly turn the puppet's head so that everyone in the audience can see the puppet's face. When you rehearse, practice focusing the puppet's eyes on the audience, on you, and on its surroundings. One way to do this is to pretend that you are seeing through the puppet's eyes. What is the puppet seeing? If you were the puppet, how would you react to what you see?

Carefully observe the movements of real animals to help you get your animal puppets to move in a realistic manner. For example, watch the pouncing and walking of a cat to help you develop realistic cat movements for manipulating a cat puppet. Observe a dog's barking or a snake's slithering and then use a mirror to observe your puppet's actions as it barks or slithers. You want your puppet's movements to be as lifelike as possible to help your audience suspend disbelief and think the puppet is alive.

As you begin telling stories with a puppet, you may want to choose material that lets you be the narrator and have the puppet act out the story events. The puppet does not have to mime all of the story action, just some of it. The puppet does not have to talk; its actions can simply complement your storytelling. Chases and other action scenes become much more entertaining when enacted by a puppet or puppets. Once you become comfortable telling stories with a puppet, try changing your voice to one appropriate for your puppet character. Subtle voice changes in tone or pace can be used to distinguish your voice from the puppet's voice. If your story involves animals, you might add animal sounds to your presentation.

Practice projecting your voice rather than shouting. To project your voice, speak from your diaphragm by pushing up air from the bottom of your lungs (Minkel, 2001). Speak naturally with hesitations and incomplete sentences. Speak slowly and distinctly to be sure those in the back of the audience can hear you and understand what you are saying. Use your natural voice as much as you can, because maintaining a character's voice is difficult. Throughout your presentation you will have to maintain the same voice for the puppet, so you want to select a voice that you can easily use each time the puppet speaks. Each puppet in the presentation will need its own voice so the audience can tell which puppet is speaking. One puppet's voice might be of a higher pitch than another puppet's voice. Match the puppet's voice to its size, age, and personality. Use a deep voice for large puppets and a high-pitched voice for small or young puppets. When the puppet is excited, talk faster and with excitement. If the puppet is bored, slow down your voice. When you are alone driving in your car, cooking in your kitchen, or working in your yard, try out different voices for your puppet. Once you decide on a voice for your puppet, tape record your presentation. As you listen to the tape, you should be able to tell the difference between your voice and the voice of the puppet (Minkel, 2001).

As the puppet speaks, open its mouth smoothly. Open and close the puppet's mouth as you open and close your own mouth. Just as you close your mouth after every word, the puppet's mouth should close after every word. Or you may decide to open the puppet's mouth only to emphasize important words. When the puppet is talking, keep it moving in a purposeful, natural manner so that it seems alive. When we speak, we move our lower jaw, so when the puppet speaks, its lower jaw should move. Use your thumb to move the lower part of the puppet's mouth. If you move the upper jaw, the puppet's head will tilt backward and it will lose eye contact with the audience. While this might happen when the puppet is laughing or sneezing, you want to minimize the amount of time the puppet is not maintaining eye contact with the audience. Practice in front of a mirror to be sure the puppet's mouth is opening and closing at the appropriate times. If the puppet is not speaking, then its mouth should be closed. We use our mouths to talk and to yawn, sneeze, cough, eat, and chew. Think about ways to naturally incorporate these actions into your presentation. To do these actions in a smooth and realistic manner, the puppet should fit loosely on your hand so that it can be easily manipulated.

Glove puppets may have a character on each finger, or the fingers of the glove may form the legs of the puppet. Glove puppets are especially useful with young children or small groups of children, who like to try them on and retell the stories to each other. Oftentimes glove puppets require you to manipulate one finger at a time. This may take some practice in order for you to hold up one or two fingers at a time. Try doing the "wave" with your fingers by moving them up and down one at a time going from left to right and then from right to left (Henson, 1994). This exercise forces you to move only one finger at a time and helps you develop the dexterity needed to manipulate a glove puppet.

REHEARSING WITH PUPPETS

Successful storytelling with hand puppets requires practice. Practicing in front of a mirror is one way to get instant feedback about your performance, and you can make adjustments as you perform. You can also videotape your performance and then review the tape to see what parts of the performance you want to work on further. Whether you rehearse in front of a mirror or videotape your rehearsal, as you watch yourself perform, determine whether the outfit you are wearing distracts from your performance. Your outfit should not be flamboyant or obtrusive; you do not want your outfit to intrude on your performance or take attention away from what you are saying and doing. As you rehearse, time your performance so you can determine how many poems and stories you will need to fill your allotted time. You may want to include an extra story in case you finish the planned stories ahead of time.

As you rehearse, try out different locations for your notes, props, books, and puppets to determine which works best for you. You might find it best to have a table alongside you where you can arrange the puppets and props in the order that you will use them. If you are going to be seated during your performance, be certain that you can easily reach your materials from where you will be seated. Prior to your performance, cover your puppets and props with a sheet or a piece of fabric. Gradually uncover them as you use them in your performance.

You do need to rehearse, but if you rehearse too much, the performance loses its spontaneity. Once you feel confident about your performance, practice it with a familiar audience such as your children, relatives, or neighborhood children. Ask them to tell you what they like and what they think you should change.

PRESENTATION

About an hour before your presentation, begin setting up your chair, table, books, props, and puppets. If you are using a microphone or any other equipment, take the time to test it and make sure it is working correctly. Arrange the area for your audience. Review your notes on the order of your presentation and quickly reread the stories or poems you will be presenting. You might find it helpful to take a quick walk outdoors or find a quiet place to breathe deeply and relax just before your performance.

You want to be close to the audience, so have them sit in a semicircle around you. Smaller children can sit on the floor in front of you, and taller children can sit in chairs behind them. This ensures that the audience will all have a good view of you and of the puppets. Minkel (2001) suggests that you gently remind children about proper audience behavior. Before you begin your presentation, explain to your audience that you expect them to sit still and that when you want them to respond or join in you will indicate that with a hand motion or a nod of your head. Alternately, you may decide to just begin with a quick poem or song that will get the audience's attention. If possible, have another adult nearby to deal with disruptive children so that you do not have to stop your performance.

Should you require a microphone, arrange for it before the program and practice using it. A clip-on lavaliere microphone is usually the best choice because it will easily pick up your voice and allow you to keep your hands free. Clip the microphone on your chest at different heights until you find the ideal location. Almost any lapel-mike will do, but be certain you practice with it before the presentation. Check the batteries to be sure they are fully charged. If you are doing the puppet show in your library with your equipment, take the time to check out the equipment and practice with it well before the performance. If you are doing the presentation in another location and not using your own microphone, be sure to visit the location and check out the equipment several days before your presentation. When you practice with the microphone, have someone sit in the back of the room to test the volume as you practice. Remember that a room full of people requires more volume than an empty room. Unless you are in a small room, do not assume that your voice will carry sufficiently without the microphone. Speak slowly and distinctly; pause if there is laughter or some auditory response from the audience.

Your audiences' attention spans will vary, so as you present, pay attention to their demeanor and adapt your presentation accordingly. You may find that you need to slow down or speed up your performance. If the audience is listening attentively and enjoying the story, you may want to elaborate on parts of the story. When you finish your presentation, give the audience time to comment on the story or ask questions about the story or the puppet.

With a puppet on your hand you will fade into the background as your audience focuses on the puppet and your story. Your enthusiasm and genuine interest in what you are doing will be noticed by the audience. If you are having fun and enjoying yourself, then your audience will also have fun and enjoy themselves. As you repeat your performances, remember that for your audience it is the first time they have seen the presentation, so remember to show your enthusiasm for the story. Your reaction to the story and interaction with your audience should be fresh and enthusiastic every time you tell the story.

STORING PUPPETS, BOOKS, AND PROPS

As your collection of puppets, books, and props grows, you can create a database to help you keep track of your materials. Puppets may be stored on puppet trees, in clear plastic bins, or in fishnet hammocks. Puppet trees make it easier to find the puppets and to see at a glance which puppets you have. If you decide to store them in bins, clearly label the bins so that you can quickly determine what is inside the bin. Allow plenty of room in the bins so the puppets do not get squashed, and include a list of the stories in which the puppets are used. The books themselves may be stored either in the bins with the puppets or on shelves located near the puppets. If you are using more than one puppet or a puppet with several props, you may want to store them in a bin so they can be kept together and easily located for the next performance. If other librarians are using the puppets, stories, and props, work with them to determine the best storage method so that everyone can locate them. Stores that sell puppets often sell racks, bins, and hammocks for storing puppets.

Once you finish a performance, check to make sure that the puppets do not need any repairs before you store them. Look for loose threads that need to be clipped or seams that need to be stitched or features that need to be glued back into place. Also, check to see if the puppet needs to be cleaned. Making repairs and cleaning the puppets after each use will help ensure that the puppets will not come apart during a presentation and will last a long time.

REFERENCES

Henson, Cheryl. 1994. *The Muppets Make Puppets*. New York: Workman Publishing.

Minkel, Walter. 2000. *How to Do "The Three Bears" with Two Hands: Performing with Puppets*. Chicago: American Library Association.

———. 2001. Pulling Strings. *School Library Journal* 47 (August): 41.

II

LEARN AND SHARE EASY PUPPET STORIES

5

VISITING CLASSIC FRIENDS

THE GOLDEN GIRLS

Nursery Rhymes

Ages 2 to 8
Time: 4 minutes

Puppet Needed

One girl puppet

Props Needed

One plush sheep for Little Bo-Peep

One spider for Little Miss Muffet

One bowl of cereal and a spoon for Miss Muffet

One small bouquet of flowers for Mistress Mary

One teakettle for Polly

One small straw doll hat for the puppet (optional)

Figure 5-1 Girl Puppet

The Stories

"Little Bo-Peep" features a careless shepherdess who has lost her sheep. In "Little Miss Muffet" a spider frightens a little girl. "Mistress Mary, Quite Contrary" is about a contrary maiden who is also a gardener. "Polly, Put the Kettle On" has two girls making tea.

Preparation Before the Puppet Show

- Locate or create the girl puppet.
- Locate the props.
- Memorize the nursery rhymes.

Before the Presentation

- Place the girl puppet on your right hand and use your left hand to pick up the props (vice versa for lefties).
- Arrange the sheep, the spider, the bowl of cereal, the bouquet of flowers, and the teakettle within easy reach.

Presentation

Little Bo-Peep

*(Introduce the girl puppet by having her wave and bow to the audience.
Pick up the sheep and hold it to the side.)*

Little Bo-Peep has lost her sheep,

(Turn the puppet to the right and left as though she is looking for her sheep.)

And doesn't know where to find them.

(As the puppet looks for the sheep, move the sheep around but not where the puppet is looking.)

Leave them alone and they'll come home,

(Move the sheep toward the puppet.)

Wagging their tails behind them.

(Put the sheep back on the table.)

Little Miss Muffet

(Have the puppet make eye contact with the audience. You may want to place a bowl of cereal in front of Miss Muffet to represent the curds and whey. Pick up the spider, but keep it concealed in your hand, or if it is a large spider, hold it behind you out of the audience's sight.)

Little Miss Muffet sat on her tuffet,

(If the puppet has a moveable arm, bring the hand to the mouth to indicate that she is eating.)

Eating her curds and whey.

(Quickly reveal the spider and place it beside the puppet.)

Along came a spider and sat down beside her,

(Have the puppet jump up and move the puppet behind your back.)

And frightened Miss Muffet away.

(Put the spider back on the table.)

Mistress Mary, Quite Contrary

(Have the puppet make eye contact with the audience. Pick up the bouquet of flowers and hold it in front of you.)

Mary, Mary quite contrary,

(Bend the puppet over the bouquet of flowers as if she is smelling them.)

How does your garden grow?

(Move the puppet's hands together near the flowers to make it seem that she is arranging them.)

With cockleshells and silver bells
And little maids all in a row.

(Have the puppet bow to the audience and put the flowers back on the table.)

Polly, Put the Kettle On

(Have the puppet make eye contact with the audience. Pick up the teakettle and hold it in front of you.)

Polly, put the kettle on,
Polly, put the kettle on,

(Move the puppet toward the teakettle.)

Polly, put the kettle on,
We'll all have tea.

Sukey, take it off again,
Sukey, take it off again,

(Move the puppet away from the teakettle.)

Sukey, take it off again,
They've all gone away.

(Have the puppet bow to the audience and wave.)

Variations

- Mother Goose nursery rhymes are part of an oral tradition, and as such there are variations in the words used in the rhymes. We have included some collections that you can consult and suggest that you read variations of the rhymes and decide on the one that you like best, which may very well be the version you remember from your childhood.

  - *Dan Yaccarino's Mother Goose*. Illustrated by Dan Yaccarino. New York: Golden Books, 2004.
  - *Mother Goose*. Arranged and edited by Eulalie Osgood Grover. Illustrated by Frederick Richardson. New York: Derrydale Books, 1997.
  - *My Very First Mother Goose*. Edited by Iona Opie. Illustrated by Rosemary Wells. Cambridge, MA: Candlewick Press, 1996.
  - *The Neighborhood Mother Goose*. Illustrated by Nina Crews. New York: Harper-Collins, 2004.
  - *Will Moses Mother Goose*. Illustrated by Will Moses. New York: Philomel, 2003.

Girl Puppet

Directions for the basic felt hand puppet that is used to make the girl puppet are included in Chapter 3 on pages 25–26. Patterns for the girl puppet are in the "Puppet Patterns Pantry" on pages 129–130. A small straw hat was added to the basic felt hand puppet.

Figure 5-2   Girl Puppet with Straw Hat

THE BOY BAND

Used for: Nursery Rhymes

Ages 2 to 8

Time: 4 minutes

Puppet Needed

One boy puppet

Props Needed

One candlestick and candle for Jack, Be Nimble

One slice of bread and butter on a plate for Little Tommy Tucker

One pie for Simple Simon. If you decide to present a longer version of the nursery rhyme, you may want to include props for each of the verses, which might be a duck, a pail, a bird, a hare, a cow, or a sieve.

One clock set at 8:00 for Wee Willie Winkie

Figure 5-3   Boy Puppet

The Stories

"Jack, Be Nimble" is about a spry youngster who jumps over a candlestick. "Little Tommy Tucker" is about a boy singing for his supper. "Simple Simon" is about a boy going to the fair asking for a taste of pie. Some versions of this tale have just two verses, and other versions have as many as ten verses. "Wee Willie Winkie" is about a young boy running through the town.

Preparation Before the Puppet Show

- Locate a boy puppet or create a boy puppet.
- Locate the props.
- Memorize the nursery rhymes.

Before the Presentation

- Place the boy puppet on your left hand so you can use your right hand to pick up the props (vice versa for lefties).
- Arrange the candle and candlestick, slice of bread and butter on a plate, pie plate, and clock in order and within easy reach.

Presentation

Jack, Be Nimble

>   *(Introduce the boy puppet by having him wave and bow to the audience.*
>   *Pick up the candlestick and hold it to your side.)*

Jack, be nimble,

>   *(Have him appear to be warming up by touching his toes, raising his arms,*
>   *jumping up and down, or boxing.)*

Jack, be quick,

>   *(Move candlestick just in front of you. Position the puppet in front of the*
>   *candlestick and bounce him up and down as he prepares for his big leap.*
>   *Move him up and over the candlestick with a big flourish.)*

Jack, jump over the candlestick.

>   *(Put the candlestick back on the table.)*

Little Tommy Tucker

>   *(Have the puppet make eye contact with the audience. Pick up the*
>   *plate of bread and butter and hold it in front of you.)*

Little Tommy Tucker
Sings for his supper.
What shall we give him?
Brown bread and butter.

>   *(Move the plate of bread and butter in front of you and have the*
>   *puppet stretch out his arms to try to reach it.)*

How shall he cut it
Without a knife?
How will he marry
Without a wife?

>   *(Have the puppet stare directly at the audience. If the puppet's head is moveable,*
>   *tilt it a bit to give it a puzzled look. Put the plate of bread and butter back on the table.)*

Simple Simon

(Have the puppet make eye contact with the audience. Pick up the pie and hold it in front of you.)

Simple Simon met a pieman

(Move the puppet around as if he is walking.)

Going to the fair.
Says Simple Simon to the pieman,

(Use the puppet's hand or head to point to the pie to indicate that he wants a taste of the pie. Use a high-pitched voice for Simon.)

Let me taste your ware.
Says the pieman to Simple Simon,

(Use a deeper voice for the pieman.)

Show me first your penny.
Says Simple Simon to the pieman,

(Have the puppet put up his empty hands or shake his head "no" to indicate he does not have a penny. Use a high-pitched voice for Simon.)

Indeed, I have not any.

(Put the pie back on the table.)

Wee Willie Winkie

(Have the puppet make eye contact with the audience. Pick up the clock and hold it in front of you. Move the puppet back and forth in front of you as though he is running.)

Wee Willie Winkie runs through the town,

(Move the puppet up and down on a diagonal to indicate he is climbing stairs.)

Upstairs and downstairs in his nightgown,

(Make a knock, knock sound with your mouth.)

Rapping at the windows, crying through the locks,

(Turn the clock face to the audience to show the time.)

Are the children all in bed? For now it's eight o'clock.

(Put the clock back on the table and have the puppet take a bow.)

Variations

- Mother Goose nursery rhymes are part of an oral tradition, and as such there are variations in the words used in the rhymes. We have included some collections that you can consult and suggest that you read variations of the rhymes and decide on the one that you like best, which may very well be the version you remember from your childhood.

  - *Dan Yaccarino's Mother Goose.* Illustrated by Dan Yaccarino. New York: Golden Books, 2004.
  - *Mother Goose.* Arranged and edited by Eulalie Osgood Grover. Illustrated by Frederick Richardson. New York: Derrydale Books, 1997.
  - *My Very First Mother Goose.* Edited by Iona Opie. Illustrated by Rosemary Wells. Cambridge, MA: Candlewick Press, 1996.
  - *The Neighborhood Mother Goose.* Illustrated by Nina Crews. New York: HarperCollins, 2004.
  - *Will Moses Mother Goose.* Illustrated by Will Moses. New York: Philomel, 2003.

Figure 5-4   Felt Boy Puppet

Boy Puppet

Materials

Two pieces of 9-inch by 12-inch blue felt for the body

Two wiggle eyes (optional)

Scraps of felt (dark brown, light brown, white, dark blue, light pink)

Pencil

Scissors

Glue gun and glue

Directions

1. Photocopy or trace the patterns in the "Puppet Patterns Pantry" on pages 129–130 to create the body of the puppet using the blue felt for the body, the light brown felt for the face and hands, and the dark brown felt for the hair. Cut the patterns out.
2. The directions for creating the basic felt hand puppet are in Chapter 3 on pages 25–26.
3. Cut the hair from the dark brown felt using the pattern in the "Puppet Patterns Pantry" on page 133.
4. Cut along the parallel lines on the hair to create bangs for the boy.
5. Glue the hair to the top of the boy's face.
6. Glue on the small oval wiggle eyes or cut small white felt ovals and small blue felt circles for the eyes. See Figure 5-6 to determine the placement of the facial features.
7. Cut a mouth from a scrap of pink felt.

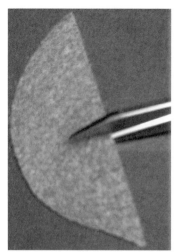

Figure 5-5   Hair

Figure 5-6   Facial Features

8. Glue on the mouth.
9. Cut out a nose from the light brown felt using the pattern in the "Puppet Patterns Pantry" on page 133.
10. Glue on the nose.
11. Set the puppet aside to let the glue dry.

OLDIES BUT GOODIES

Old MacDonald Had a Farm

Folk Song

Ages 3 to 10
Time: 5 minutes

Purchasing Puppets Tips

For this popular children's song you can find Old MacDonald hand puppet sets and finger puppet sets that come with a farmer and five to eleven farm animals. An advantage to buying the set is that the puppets can all be used for a variety of puppet presentations. This song is especially appropriate for a glove puppet with Old McDonald on the thumb and one animal on each of the fingers. Rather than purchasing a set, you may want to consider purchasing a man or boy puppet and four or five farm animal puppets to use in this presentation. You can include as many farm animal puppets as you have and add to you collection as you find suitable farm animal puppets. Because the farm animals do not have to move, you can use stuffed animals in the presentation rather than puppets.

Figure 5-7   Old MacDonald

Puppets Needed

One farmer puppet

Props Needed

One each: cat, dog, sheep, cow, horse

The Story

Old MacDonald and his noisy farm animals have enchanted young audiences for years. The rollicking chorus of E-I-E-I-O sets a lively tone for this presentation.

Preparation Before the Puppet Show

- Locate or create the puppet.
- Locate or create the props.
- Arrange the cat, dog, sheep, cow, and horse in the correct order within easy reach.
- If you are using a glove puppet, place it on your dominant hand with your palm facing you and all the fingers lowered toward you.

As the song begins, raise your thumb with the farmer attached. Raise each finger in turn to show the animals.

Presentation

Old MacDonald Had a Farm

> *(Introduce Old MacDonald by having him wave and bow to the audience.)*

> Old MacDonald had a farm, E-I-E-I-O.
> And on that farm he had a

> *(Hold up the cat, have it scan the audience, and wait for the children to say its name.)*

> cat.

> *(Say "cat" with the children. Encourage the children to join you by using a hand motion, nodding at them, or looking at them expectantly.)*

> With a "meow, meow" here and a "meow, meow" there,
> Here a "meow," there a "meow,"
> Everywhere a "meow, meow."
> Old MacDonald had a farm, E-I-E-I-O.

> *(Have the cat take a quick bow and put it behind you.)*

> Old MacDonald had a farm, E-I-E-I-O.
> And on that farm he had a

> *(Hold up the dog, have it scan the audience, and wait for the children to say its name.)*

> dog.

> *(Say "dog" with the children. Encourage the children to join you by using a hand motion, nodding at them, or looking at them expectantly.)*

> With a "bow wow" here and a "bow wow" there,
> Here a "bow wow," there a "bow wow,"
> Everywhere a "bow wow."
> Old MacDonald had a farm, E-I-E-I-O.

> *(Have the dog take a quick bow and put it behind you.)*

> Old MacDonald had a farm, E-I-E-I-O.
> And on that farm he had a

(Hold up the sheep, have it scan the audience, and wait for the children to say its name.)

sheep.

(Say "sheep" with the children. Encourage the children to join you by using a hand motion, nodding at them, or looking at them expectantly.)

With a "baa, baa" here and a "baa, baa" there,
Here a "baa," there a "baa,"
Everywhere a "baa, baa."
Old MacDonald had a farm, E-I-E-I-O.

(Have the sheep take a quick bow and put it behind you.)

Old MacDonald had a farm, E-I-E-I-O.
And on that farm he had a

(Hold up the cow, have it scan the audience, and wait for the children to say its name.)

cow.

(Say "cow" with the children. Encourage the children to join you by using a hand motion, nodding at them, or looking at them expectantly.)

With a "moo, moo" here and a "moo, moo" there,
Here a "moo," there a "moo,"
Everywhere a "moo, moo."
Old MacDonald had a farm, E-I-E-I-O.

(Have the cow take a quick bow and put it behind you.)

Old MacDonald had a farm, E-I-E-I-O.
And on that farm he had a

(Hold up the horse, have it scan the audience, and wait for the children to say its name.)

horse.

(Say "horse" with the children. Encourage the children to join you by using a hand motion, nodding at them, or looking at them expectantly.)

With a "neigh, neigh" here and a "neigh, neigh" there,
Here a "neigh," there a "neigh,"
Everywhere a "neigh, neigh."
Old MacDonald had a farm, E-I-E-I-O.

(Have the horse take a quick bow, put it behind you, and end with a final rousing chorus of)

Old MacDonald had a farm, E-I-E-I-O.

Variations

• Find lyrics to the song on the Internet at http://www.niehs.nih.gov/kids/lyrics/mcdonald.htm and http://www.songsforteaching.com/folk/oldmacdonaldhadafarm.htm.
• Storybook versions:

  • *Old MacDonald Had a Farm.* Illustrated by Glen Rounds. New York: Holiday House, 1989.
  • *Old MacDonald Had a Farm.* Illustrated by Holly Berry. New York: North-South, 1994.
  • Schwartz, Amy. *Old MacDonald Had a Farm.* New York: Scholastic, 1999.
  • Yolen, Jane. *Jane Yolen's Old MacDonald Songbook.* Illustrated by Rosekrans Hoffman. Honesdate, PA: Boyds Mills, 1994.

• Sing about other animals on the farm or perhaps machines on the farm that make noises such as a tractor or a pickup truck.

Old MacDonald Puppet

Materials

Two pieces of 9-inch by 12-inch dark blue felt for the body

One piece of 2-inch by 5-inch dark brown felt for the hat

One piece of 3-inch by 3-inch yellow felt for Old MacDonald's scarf

One piece of 5-inch by 5-inch light pink or light brown felt for Old MacDonald's face and hands

Scraps of white and blue felt for the eyes

Scrap of pink or red felt for the mouth

Wiggle eyes (optional)

Glue gun and glue

Scissors

Figure 5-8 Felt Old MacDonald Puppet

Figure 5-9   Old MacDonald Eyes and Mouth

Directions

THE BODY

1. Photocopy or trace the patterns in the "Puppet Patterns Pantry" on pages 129–130 for the body of the puppet and the facial features. Cut out the patterns.
2. Cut the body from the dark blue felt.
3. Cut the face and hands from the light brown felt or light pink felt.
4. Cut the felt eyes from the white and blue felt.
5. Cut a mouth from the red felt.
6. Follow the directions in Chapter 3 on pages 25–26 for a basic felt hand puppet.

THE HAT, THE MOUSTACHE, AND THE SCARF

1. Photocopy or trace the patterns for the hat, the moustache, and the scarf in the "Puppet Patterns Pantry" on page 134. Cut out the patterns.
2. Cut the hat from the dark brown felt.
3. Glue the hat on the top of Old MacDonald's head. (See Figure 5-10.)
4. Cut the moustache from the white felt.
5. Glue the moustache just above the mouth. (See Figure 5-10.)
6. Cut the scarf from the yellow felt.
7. Glue the scarf just below Old MacDonald's face.

Figure 5-10   Old MacDonald Hat, Moustache, and Scarf

Farm Animal Props

Figure 5-11   Farm Animal Props

Materials

One piece of 9-inch by 12-inch dark brown felt for the dog and horse bodies

One piece of 9-inch by 12-inch light brown felt for the cow, the dog's ears and tail, and the horse's mane and tail

One piece of 9-inch by 12-inch white felt for the cat, the sheep, and the cow's horns

Scraps of black felt for the animals' eyes

Scraps of pink felt for the animals' noses

Five craft sticks

Glue gun and glue

Craft glue

Scissors

Thin black marker

Directions

Follow the directions for the stick puppets on pages 31–32 in Chapter 3.

THE CAT

1. Photocopy or trace the patterns for the cat in the "Puppet Patterns Pantry" on page 135. Cut out the patterns.
2. Cut the cat from light brown felt.
3. Cut two small blue circles for the cat's eyes.

4. Glue the eyes on the cat's face.
5. Cut a small black felt triangle for the cat's nose.
6. Glue the nose on just below the eyes.
7. Cut two tiny pink felt triangles to line the cat's ears.
8. Glue the pink triangles to the ears.
9. Draw a line with a thin black permanent marker just under the cat's face to separate it from the body.
10. Glue a craft stick to the back of the cat.

THE DOG

1. Photocopy or trace the pattern for the dog, the dog's tail, and the dog's ears in the "Puppet Patterns Pantry" on page 135. Cut out the patterns.
2. Cut the dog from the dark brown felt.
3. Cut the dog's tail from the light brown felt.
4. Glue on the dog's tail.
5. Cut the dog's ears from the light brown felt.
6. Glue the ears on the dog's head.
7. Cut two small black felt circles for the dog's eyes.
8. Glue the eyes on the dog's face.
9. Cut a small pink felt triangle for the dog's nose.
10. Glue the nose on just below the eyes.
11. Use a thin black marker to draw a line just under the dog's face to separate it from the body.
12. Glue a craft stick to the back of the dog.

THE SHEEP

1. Photocopy or trace the pattern for the sheep's body and the sheep's ears in the "Puppet Patterns Pantry" on page 136. Cut out the patterns.
2. Cut the sheep from the white felt.
3. Cut two sheep ears from the white felt.
4. Glue the ears to the top of the head.
5. Cut two small black circles for the sheep's eyes.
6. Glue the eyes on the sheep's face.
7. Cut a small pink triangle for the sheep's nose.
8. Glue the nose on just below the eyes.
9. Glue a craft stick to the back of the sheep.

THE COW

1. Photocopy or trace the patterns for the cow, the cow's tail, and the cow's horns in the "Puppet Patterns Pantry" on page 136. Cut out the patterns.
2. Cut the cow and the cow's tail from light brown felt.
3. Cut the cow's horns from white felt.
4. Glue on the cow's horns.
5. Cut a small oval from light pink felt for the cow's snout.
6. Glue the snout on the cow's head.
7. Cut two small black felt circles for the cow's eyes.

8. Glue the eyes on the cow's face.
9. Use the thin black marker to draw a line just under the cow's face to separate it from the body.
10. Make two black marks on the cow's snout for the nostrils.
11. Glue a craft stick to the back of the cow.

THE HORSE

1. Photocopy or trace the patterns for the horse, the horse's mane, and the horse's tail in the "Puppet Patterns Pantry" on page 137. Cut out the patterns.
2. Cut the horse from dark brown felt.
3. Cut the horse's mane from the light brown felt.
4. Glue on the horse's mane.
5. Cut the horse's tail from the light brown felt.
6. Glue on the tail.
7. Cut one small black felt circle for the horse's eye.
8. Glue the eye on the horse's face.
9. Glue a craft stick to the back of the horse.

The Old Lady Who Swallowed a Fly

Folk Song

Ages 2 and up
Time: 20 minutes

Puppets Needed

One old lady puppet with a mouth that opens wide enough to swallow the props and a stomach large enough to hold them.

Props Needed

One each: fly, spider, bird, cat, dog, goat, cow, and horse.

When gathering the props, try to have them in proportion to each other. For example, the dog should be smaller than the horse.

The Story

An old lady swallows a fly, then swallows a spider to catch the fly, and so the story begins. She swallows a succession of animals each larger than the last one, confident that each will catch the one before.

Preparation Before the Puppet Show

• Locate or create the old lady puppet.
• Locate or create the props.

- Arrange the fly, spider, bird, cat, dog, goat, cow, and horse in the correct order within easy reach.
- Memorize this simple rhyming refrain: "I don't know why she swallowed the fly. Poor old lady, she'll probably die."

Before the Presentation

- Place the old lady puppet on your left hand so you can use your right hand to put the animals into her mouth (vice versa for lefties).
- Tell your audience to

  - Call out the name of the different animals as you hold them up, and
  - Join you for the repeated refrain: "Poor old lady, she'll probably die."

- Begin by saying the whole refrain the first time.

Presentation

There was an old lady

(Introduce the old lady puppet by having her wave and bow to the audience.)

who swallowed a

(Hold up the fly and wait for the children to say its name.)

fly.

(Say "fly" with the children and put the fly inside the old lady.)

I don't know why she swallowed the fly. Poor old lady, she'll probably die.

*(Encourage the children to join you as you say the refrain by using
a hand motion, nodding at them, or looking at them expectantly.)*

There was an old lady who swallowed a

(Hold up the spider and wait for the children to say its name.)

spider.

(Say "spider" with the children and put the spider inside the old lady.)

That wiggled and jiggled and tickled inside her.
She swallowed the spider to catch the fly.
I don't know why she swallowed the fly. Poor old lady, she'll probably die.

(Encourage the children to join you as you say the refrain by using a hand motion, nodding at them, or looking at them expectantly.)

There was an old lady who swallowed a

(Hold up the bird and wait for the children to say its name.)

bird.

(Say "bird" with the children and put the bird inside the old lady.)

How absurd to swallow a bird.
She swallowed the bird to catch the spider
That wiggled and jiggled and tickled inside her.
She swallowed the spider to catch the fly.
I don't know why she swallowed the fly. Poor old lady, she'll probably die.

(Encourage the children to join you as you say the refrain by using a hand motion, nodding at them, or looking at them expectantly.)

There was an old lady who swallowed a

(Hold up the cat and wait for the children to say its name.)

cat.

(Say "cat" with the children and put the cat inside the old lady.)

Imagine that, she swallowed a cat.
She swallowed the cat to catch the bird.
She swallowed the bird to catch the spider
That wiggled and jiggled and tickled inside her.
She swallowed the spider to catch the fly.
I don't know why she swallowed the fly. Poor old lady, she'll probably die.

(Encourage the children to join you as you say the refrain by using a hand motion, nodding at them, or looking at them expectantly.)

There was an old lady who swallowed a

(Hold up the dog and wait for the children to say its name.)

dog.

(Say "dog" with the children and put the dog inside the old lady.)

What a hog! She swallowed a dog!
She swallowed the dog to catch the cat.
She swallowed the cat to catch the bird.
She swallowed the bird to catch the spider
That wiggled and jiggled and tickled inside her.
She swallowed the spider to catch the fly.
I don't know why she swallowed the fly. Poor old lady, she'll probably die.

(Encourage the children to join you as you say the refrain by using
a hand motion, nodding at them, or looking at them expectantly.)

There was an old lady who swallowed a

(Hold up the goat and wait for the children to say its name.)

goat.

Say "goat" with the children and put the goat inside the old lady.

She opened her throat and swallowed a goat.
She swallowed the goat to catch the dog.
She swallowed the dog to catch the cat.
She swallowed the cat to catch the bird.
She swallowed the bird to catch the spider
That wiggled and jiggled and tickled inside her.
She swallowed the spider to catch the fly.
I don't know why she swallowed the fly. Poor old lady, she'll probably die.

(Encourage the children to join you as you say the refrain by using
a hand motion, nodding at them, or looking at them expectantly.)

There was an old lady who swallowed a

(Hold up the cow and wait for the children to say its name.)

cow.

(Say "cow" with the children and put the cow inside the old lady.)

I don't know how she swallowed a cow.
She swallowed the cow to catch the goat.
She swallowed the goat to catch the dog.
She swallowed the dog to catch the cat.
She swallowed the cat to catch the bird.
She swallowed the bird to catch the spider
That wiggled and jiggled and tickled inside her.

She swallowed the spider to catch the fly.
I don't know why she swallowed the fly. Poor old lady, she'll probably die.

(Encourage the children to join you as you say the refrain by using a hand motion, nodding at them, or looking at them expectantly.)

There was an old lady who swallowed a

(Hold up the horse and wait for the children to say its name.)

horse.

(Say "horse" with the children and put the horse inside the old lady. Slowly say the closing line.)

She died of course.

Collapse the old lady into your lap to indicate that she died.

Variations

• Have the children shout out the animals' sounds rather than their names.

   • Suggest a sound or perhaps a motion for the spider. Use the finger play motion of the spider climbing the waterspout from "The Itsy Bitsy Spider."

• Find other versions of the folk song on the Internet at http://www.niehs.nih.gov/kids/lyrics/oldlady.htm.
• Storybook versions

   • Karas, G. Brian. *I Know an Old Lady*. New York: Scholastic, 1994.
   • Rounds, Glen. *I Know an Old Lady Who Swallowed a Fly*. New York: Holiday House, 1990.
   • Taback, Simms. *There Was an Old Lady Who Swallowed a Fly*. New York: Viking, 1997.

Old Lady Puppet

Materials

Two pieces of 9-inch by 12-inch dark pink felt

One piece of 5-inch by 6-inch light pink felt

Scraps of felt (white, blue, black, dark brown, light brown, light pink, red)

One 6-inch piece of lace

One 6-inch piece of 5⁄8-inch white ribbon

Two small buttons

Wiggle eyes or scraps of white and blue felt for the eyes

Figure 5-12 Old Lady Puppet and Animal Props

Plastic sandwich bag

Glue gun and glue

Scissors

Directions

1. Photocopy or trace the patterns in the "Puppet Patterns Pantry" on pages 129–130 for the body of the puppet using the dark pink felt for the dress, the light brown felt or light pink felt for the face and hands, and the red felt for the mouth. Cut out the patterns.
2. Photocopy or trace the patterns in the "Puppet Patterns Pantry" on pages 138–139 to create the hair using the white felt and the apron of the puppet using the light pink felt. Cut out the patterns.
3. Cut out body, face, hands, mouth, hair, and apron.
4. Follow the directions in Chapter 3 on pages 25–26 for a basic felt hand puppet.

THE BODY

1. Cut a 2-inch by 3-inch hole 3 inches from the bottom of the front body piece. (See Figure 5-13.)

   • Use the hole for slipping the animals in and out.
   • An apron will cover the hole.

2. Glue on the face, hands, and hair on the front body piece.

3. Glue on the mouth and the small oval wiggle eyes or cut small white felt ovals and small blue felt circles for the eyes. (See Figure 5-14.)

4. Set the puppet aside for the glue to dry.

5. Turn the front body piece over and glue the plastic sandwich bag just over the hole. (See Figure 5-15.)

   • When you tell the story, you will simply lift the apron to insert the animals.

6. Turn the ends of the lace under and glue or sew the lace to the bottom of the apron. (See Figure 5-16.)

7. Glue the apron on the front body piece over the hole.

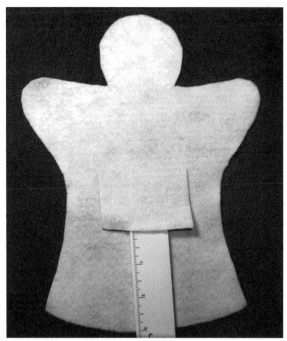

Figure 5-13   Old Lady Body with Hole

8. Glue the ribbon over the top of the apron.

9. Fold the ends of the ribbon under the front body piece and glue them down.

10. Sew the two small buttons to the front body piece, lining them up just under the mouth.

11. Glue the back of the hair to the second body piece. (See Figure 5-17.)

Figure 5-14   Face, Hands, and Hair

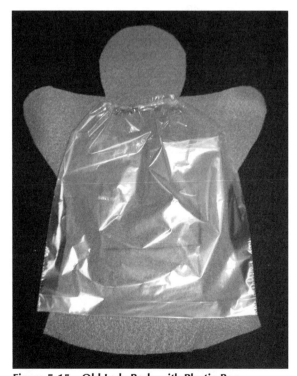

Figure 5-15   Old Lady Body with Plastic Bag

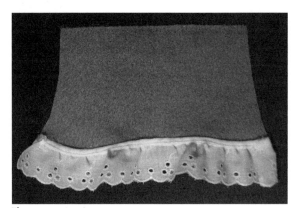

Figure 5-16   Apron

Figure 5-17   Old Lady Back

12. Glue the front piece of the puppet to the back piece, leaving the bottom open for you to insert your hand.

Animal Props

Materials

One piece of 9-inch by 12-inch dark brown felt for the dog and the horse bodies

One piece of 9-inch by 12-inch light brown felt for the cat, the cow, the dog's ears and tail, and the horse's mane and tail

One piece of 9-inch by 12-inch white felt for the cat, the goat, the cow's horns, the fly's wings, the spider's eyes, and the bird's wing

Scrap of light blue felt for the bird

Scraps of black felt for the body of the fly, the spider, and the eyes of the animals

Wiggle eyes (optional)

Glue gun and glue

Scissors

Thin black marker

Directions

Photocopy or trace the patterns in the "Puppet Patterns Pantry" on pages 135–140 for the animal props. Cut out the patterns.

THE FLY

1. Cut the fly from the black felt.
2. Cut the two wings from the white felt.
3. Glue the wings on the fly.

THE SPIDER

1. Cut the spider from the black felt.
2. Glue two very tiny wiggle eyes on the spider or cut small white felt circles for the eyes.
3. Glue the eyes on the spider.

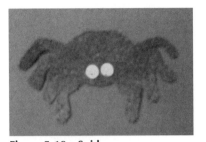

Figure 5-18   Spider

THE BIRD

1. Cut the bird from blue felt.
2. Cut the wing from white felt.
3. Glue the wing on the bird.
4. Glue one very tiny wiggle eye on the bird or cut a small black felt circle for the eye.
5. Glue the eye on the bird.

THE GOAT

1. Cut the goat from white felt and a small triangle nose from pink felt.
2. Glue two very tiny wiggle eyes on the goat or cut two small black felt circles for the eyes.
3. Glue the eyes on the goat's face.
4. Glue the nose on the goat's face just below the eyes.
5. Use a thin black marker to draw a line just under the goat's face to separate it from the body.

THE CAT, DOG, COW, AND HORSE

1. Follow the directions for the cat, dog, cow, and horse in "Old MacDonald Had a Farm" on pages 57–59.
2. Omit the craft sticks from the directions.

A FROG, THREE GOATS, AND A TROLL

The Frog Prince

Fairy Tale

Ages 5 to 12
Time: 10 minutes

Puppets Needed

One girl puppet with a crown
One frog puppet
One boy puppet with a crown (optional)

Figure 5-19   Princess and Frog

Props Needed

One golden ball
One plate
One small table
One small pillow (optional)

The Story

A frog agrees to retrieve a princess's golden ball from a well if she will take him home with her. After spending three nights in the castle with the princess, the frog becomes a prince.

Preparation Before the Puppet Show

• Locate or create the puppets.
• Locate the props.
• Arrange the ball and the prince puppet on a table beside you.
• Place the plate on a small table in front of you.

Before the Presentation

• Place the princess puppet on your left hand and the frog puppet on your right hand (vice versa for lefties).
• You do not need a king puppet; just use a deep voice for his lines.

Presentation

Narrator:
This is the story of a princess who was playing with her golden ball near the well. Now, she had been told not to play around the well, but she did anyway.

(Show the audience the princess puppet. Have the puppet make eye contact with the audience by quickly scanning the children's faces. The princess then tosses the ball up with her mouth and catches it a time or two. Then, have her drop it on a table or the floor.)

Narrator:
And so while she was playing with her golden ball it fell into the well. Oh, she was so distressed. That was her favorite, favorite ball. She had only one golden ball and she wanted so much to play with it. She sat on the edge of the well and cried.

(Have the princess cry loudly. [Audiences enjoy really exaggerated crying.])

Narrator:
While she was crying, a frog hopped up to her.

Frog:
Princess, why are you crying?

Princess:
I dropped my golden ball into the well and I can't get it.

(Move the frog nearer to the princess.)

Frog:
I'll get it for you. What will you give me for getting the ball?

Princess:
My gold bracelet.

Frog:
No. I don't want a gold bracelet. I can't use that.

Princess:
I'll give you my diamond necklace.

Frog:
No, I can't use that either. I'll tell you what I want. I will get your golden ball if you let me go home with you, eat supper with you, and sit on your pillow when you go to sleep at night and you'll be my friend.

Princess:
Oh, okay, Frog, anything. Get me my ball!

(The princess is so excited she jumps up and down.)

Narrator:
And so the frog got her ball for her. He jumped in the well, picked up
the golden ball, and gave it back to the princess.

*(The frog picks up the ball in his mouth and gives it to the princess.
She takes the ball in her mouth or hands.)*

Narrator:
The princess was so excited she grabbed the ball and ran back to the palace.

*(Quickly move the princess puppet off in either direction and put
her behind your back. Make the frog hop slowly after her and then give up.
Place the frog behind your back. Bring the princess out and
put her in front of the table with the plate.)*

Narrator:
Now, when she got back to the palace, she forgot about the frog.
She was sitting at her table eating when someone banged on the front door.

(Make a knocking sound with your mouth or knock on a table.)

Narrator:
Knock, knock, KNOCK, KNOCK.

(You do not need a king puppet, just his voice, as he is off-stage.)

King:
Who's that banging on the front door?

Princess:
Oh, it is some silly frog who thinks he is going to come in here
and eat with me and sleep on my pillow.

King:
Why would he think that?

Princess:
I told him that if he would get me my ball from the well he could come and eat with us.

King:
Well, if you told him that he can, then he can. You're a princess. You are royalty.
Always tell the truth and always keep your word.

Narrator:
Now the princess was a little disturbed by what he said, but she did as she was told.

*(Move the princess to the frog and have her open an imaginary door.
The princess nods or motions to the frog. Have the princess and the frog
move toward the plate. Raise and lower the frog's head over the plate as
though he is eating. Lower the princess's head to have her appear miserable.)*

Narrator:
All through dinner the frog looked longingly at the princess.
When she finished eating she got up to go up the stairs to bed.

King:
Where are you going?

(Use a cross and petulant voice for the princess's reply.)

Princess:
I'm going to bed.

Frog:
I get to sleep on your pillow.

King:
Why does he think that?

Princess:
Well, I sort of told him he could.

King:
Princess, you keep your word.

Narrator:
So she took the frog up the stairs, put him on her pillow, and lay down to go to sleep.

*(Lay the princess and the frog side by side on your lap or on a pillow.
The princess cries herself to sleep.)*

Princess:
Boo hoo.

*(Move the frog behind your back. Lift the princess up and have her
look around astonished that the frog is not there.)*

Princess:
Well, thank goodness he's gone. Now I can have a pleasant day!

Narrator:
But that night the frog was back for supper and to sleep on her pillow.

*(Bring the frog out from behind your back and lay the frog and the princess down together.
This time the princess isn't crying.)*

Narrator:
And the same thing happened the third night. By now the princess was no longer cross and
developed a fondness for the frog. But the morning after the third night, the frog
was not there, and in his place was a handsome prince.

*(If you use a boy puppet for the prince, drop frog off your hand and put the prince puppet on your
hand. Have the princess and prince face each other. If no prince puppet is used, say.)*

Prince:
Oh, Princess, I have been under the spell of a wicked witch. Only by sleeping on the pillow
of a real princess could the spell be broken and I could be myself again. Thank you for
letting me break the spell. I am forever indebted to you!

(The puppets hug one another.)

Narrator:
And the prince and princess were great childhood friends, and when they grew up they were married
and they lived happily ever after. And that is the story of the Frog Prince.

(Puppets bow toward the audience.)

Variations

- Find a version of this fairy tale on the Internet at http://www.eastoftheweb.com/short-stories.UBooks/FrogPrin.shtml.
- Storybook versions

  - Philip, Neil, reteller. *The Illustrated Book of Fairy Tales*. Illustrated by Nilesh Mistry. New York: DK Publishing, 1998.
  - dePaola, Tomie, reteller. *Tomie dePaola's Favorite Nursery Tales*. New York: G. P. Putnam's Sons, 1986.

Figure 5-20 Frog, Prince, and Princess Sock Puppets

Frog

Materials

One green sock

Two large round wiggle eyes

Two white 1½-inch pompoms for the frog's eyes

Thin cardboard for forming the mouth

Scissors

Glue gun and glue

Directions

1. Follow the directions in Chapter 3 on pages 30–31 for a basic sock puppet using a green sock.
2. Glue the round wiggle eyes on each of the pompoms.
3. Put the sock on your hand with the heel of the sock facing upward.
4. Scrunch up the heel of the sock and glue the pompoms with the wiggle eyes onto the heel.

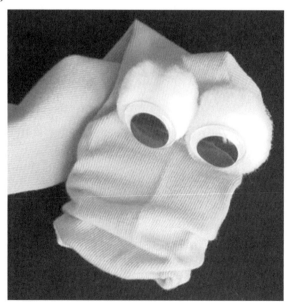

Figure 5-21 Frog Sock Puppet

Princess and Prince Puppets

Figure 5-22   Princess and Prince Sock Puppets

Materials

Two tube socks, one for the princess and one for the prince

Four small wiggle eyes for princess and prince

Two small pompoms for noses

Twelve pieces of textured yarn, each 18 inches long, for princess's hair

Two pieces of textured yarn, each 5 inches long, for princess's hair

Nine pieces of textured yarn, each 6 inches long, for prince's hair

Two pieces of thin pink ribbon, 12 inches long

Thin cardboard for forming the mouths and making the crowns

Aluminum foil

Ruler

Scissors

Glue gun and glue

Pencil

Directions

1. Follow the directions in Chapter 3 on pages 30–31 to create two basic sock puppets using the white tube socks.
2. The pattern for the crown is in the "Puppet Patterns Pantry" on page 141.

THE PRINCESS'S HAIR

1. For the princess's hair, fold the twelve pieces of 18-inch-long yarn in half.
2. Tie the yarn together with the two 5-inch pieces of yarn. (See Figure 5-23.)
3. Unravel the ends of the short pieces of yarn to make bangs.
4. Divide the twelve pieces of yarn into three groups of four and braid them to make pigtails.
5. Cut the ribbon into two pieces, each twelve inches long.
6. Tie the ends of the braids with the pieces of ribbon. (See Figure 5-24.)
7. Put a dot of glue on the knot to make sure it holds.
8. Tie the ribbons into bows. (See Figure 5-24.)
9. Measure one inch above the eyes to determine the placement of the braids.
10. Glue the braids on one of the sock puppets. You may find it helpful to put the sock on your hand and then glue on the braids.

Figure 5-23   Princess's Hair

Figure 5-24   Princess's Braid with Bow

THE PRINCE'S HAIR

1. Fold eight pieces of the 6-inch-long yarn in half.
2. Use the other piece of 6-inch-long yarn to tie the pieces together in the center. (See Figure 5-25.)
3. Glue the short hair on the other sock puppet.
4. Measure one inch above the eyes to determine the placement of the hair.
   You may find it helpful to put the sock on your hand and then glue on the hair.

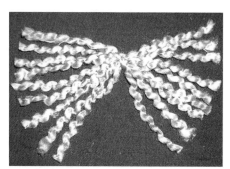

Figure 5-25   Prince's Hair

THE CROWNS

1. Trace or photocopy the crown pattern in the "Puppet Patterns Pantry" on page 141. Cut out the pattern.
2. Place the crown pattern on the thin cardboard and trace around the pattern twice.
3. Cut the two crowns out of the thin cardboard.
4. Place one crown in the center of a 9-inch by 5-inch piece of aluminum foil with the dull side facing up.
5. Turn up one half-inch of the foil over the bottom of the crown. (See Figure 5-26.)
6. Cut the foil between each point of the crown. (See Figure 5-26.)
7. Bend the foil over the cardboard crown points and trim off the extra foil at the points.
8. Glue the ends of the crowns together with hot glue.
9. Press the ends together and hold them for a few seconds for the glue to dry.
10. Use hot glue to attach the crowns to the heads of the puppets. You may find it helpful to put the sock on your hand and then glue on the hair and the crown.

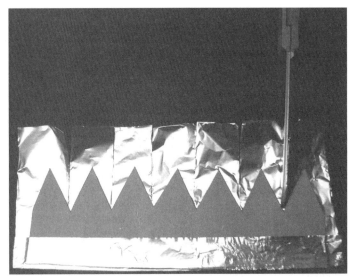

Figure 5-26   Crown with Cuts

Figure 5-27   Back of Crown

Purchasing Puppets Tips

Three billy goat puppets of different sizes and one troll are required for this presentation. Sometimes you can find all four puppets sold together in one set rather than having to search for three billy goat puppets of different sizes and a troll. If you cannot find three different-size billy goat puppets, just use one puppet and the changes in your voice will indicate that each goat is larger than the last one the troll encountered.

The Three Billy Goats Gruff

Folk Tale

Ages 3 and up
Time: 10 minutes

Puppets Needed

Three billy goats of different sizes
One troll

The Story

A wicked troll threatens a billy goat family as they try to cross a bridge to get to some sweet, green grass, but the troll is no match for the biggest billy goat.

Preparation Before the Puppet Show

- Locate or create the puppets.
- Practice the voices you will use for the three billy goats and the troll, as different vocalizations for each character are the secret to the success of this story.

Before the Presentation

- Line the billy goat puppets up on a table from smallest to largest.

Presentation

Narrator:
Once, many years ago, there lived a small family of billy goats named Gruff.

(Introduce each billy goat to the audience, one at a time. Have each puppet bow.)

Narrator:

They loved to eat sweet, green grass more than anything else. The best sweet, green grass
to be found was over the river on the side of the mountain. But the only way to
cross the river was over a small bridge, and under this bridge lived
a ferocious troll who would let nothing or no one cross the bridge.

(Do not bring the puppet up to the audience but have him growl loudly, off-stage.)

Troll:

Growllll! Growlll!

Narrator:

But the brothers were determined to try. The first billy goat to cross the
bridge was the youngest, Baby Billy Goat. Trip-trap, trip-trap, trip-trap.

*(Start the baby billy goat across the imaginary bridge. Have troll LEAP out
from under the bridge shouting in a terrible, loud roar.)*

Troll:

WHO'S THAT TRIPPING OVER MY BRIDGE?

*(Baby Billy Goat Gruff speaks in a quiet, quavering voice, very frightened.
Shake puppet as in fear of the troll.)*

Baby Billy Goat:

It is I, Mr. Troll, Baby Billy Goat Gruff. I just want to cross the
bridge to get to the grass on the side of the mountain.

(The troll speaks in harsh bullying voice.)

Troll:

This is MY bridge and I say who can cross it and I am going to eat you up!

*(Baby Billy Goat Gruff speaks in a quiet, quavering voice, very frightened.
Shake puppet as in fear of the troll.)*

Baby Billy Goat:

Oh, please, Mr. Troll, please don't eat me up! Wait for my bigger brother
who comes after me. He is much bigger than I am and will taste better!

Troll:

All right. I'll wait, but hurry on out of here.

(Move Baby Billy Goat Gruff across the bridge.)

Narrator:
Trip-trap, trip-trap, trip-trap.

(Remove Baby Billy Goat Gruff and bring up the middle-size billy goat.)

Narrator:
When Bigger Billy Goat Gruff got to the bridge he was louder. Trip-Trap, Trip-Trap, Trip-Trap!

(Start Bigger Billy Goat Gruff across the imaginary bridge. Have the troll LEAP out from under the bridge shouting in a terrible, loud roar.)

Troll:
WHO'S THAT TRIPPING OVER MY BRIDGE?

(The troll LEAPS out from under bridge with a terrible GROWL. Bigger Billy Goat Gruff speaks in a moderate voice, a little frightened.)

Bigger Billy Goat:
It is I, Mr. Troll, Bigger Billy Goat Gruff. I just want to cross the bridge to get to the grass on the side of the mountain.

(The troll speaks in harsh bullying voice.)

Troll:
This is MY bridge and I say who can cross it and I am going to eat you up!

(Bigger Billy Goat Gruff is still frightened and is shaking slightly.)

Bigger Billy Goat:
Oh, please, Mr. Troll, please don't eat me up! Wait for my bigger brother who comes after me. He is much bigger than I am and will taste better!

Troll:
All right. I'll wait, but hurry on out of here.

Narrator:
Bigger Billy Goat Gruff went on across the bridge, making slightly more noise than his little brother. Trip-Trap, Trip-Trap, Trip-Trap.

(Walk Bigger Billy Goat Gruff across the bridge a little more noisily. Remove Bigger Billy Goat Gruff and bring up the biggest billy goat.)

Narrator:
And then coming slowly and heavily was Biggest Billy Goat Gruff. He crossed the bridge loudly! TRIP-TRAP, TRIP-TRAP, TRIP-TRAP!

(Walk Biggest Billy Goat Gruff heavily and NOISILY across bridge.)

Troll:
WHO'S THAT TRIPPING OVER MY BRIDGE?

(The troll LEAPS from under the bridge with a terrible GROWL!
Biggest Billy Goat Gruff speaks in a loud, rough voice, not frightened at all.)

Biggest Billy Goat:
It is I, Troll, Biggest Billy Goat Gruff. I'm going to cross the bridge
to get to the grass on the side of the mountain.

(The troll leaps out roaring loudly and speaking in a harsh bullying voice.)

Troll:
This is MY bridge and I say who can cross it and I am going to eat you up!

Biggest Billy Goat:
Yeah? You and who else? I've got big horns to stab you with and big
hooves to kick you with and I'm going to put you in the river!

(Biggest Billy Goat Gruff stabs and kicks the troll into river. Remove the troll.)

Narrator:
And that's exactly what he did, and then he joined his brothers on the side of the mountain.

(Walk the biggest billy goat puppet across the bridge, noisily.)

Narrator:
And that's the story of "The Three Billy Goats Gruff."

Variations

- Finch, Mary, reteller. *The Three Billy Goats Gruff*. Illustrated by Roberta Arenson. New York: Barefoot Books, 2001.
- French, Vivian. *The Kingfisher Book of Nursery Tales*. Illustrated by Stephen Lambert. Boston: Kingfisher, 2003.
- Salley, Coleen, reteller. *Who's That Tripping Over My Bridge?* Illustrated by Amy Jackson Dixon. Gretna, LA: Pelican, 2002.
- Stevens, Janet, reteller. *The Three Billy Goats Gruff*. San Diego: Harcourt Brace Jovanovich, 1987.
- Yolen, Jane, reteller. *Once Upon a Bedtime Story*. Honesdale, PA: Boyds Mills, 1997.

Troll and Billy Goat Puppets

Materials

One sheet heavy paper

Four craft sticks

Glue

Markers

Scissors

Directions

1. Photocopy or trace the patterns in the "Puppet Patterns Pantry" on pages 142, 143, and 144 for the three billy goats and the troll.
2. Color them with the markers or leave them white.
3. Cut them out.
4. Glue the three billy goats and the troll to the craft sticks. (See Figure 5-28.)

Figure 5-28   Troll and Billy Goats Stick Puppets

DYNAMIC DUOS

The Lion and the Mouse

Fable

Ages 6 to 10
Time: 5 minutes

Puppets Needed

One lion puppet
One mouse puppet

Figure 5-29   Lion and Mouse Puppets

Prop Needed

One piece of rope or a net (optional)

The Story

A mouse awakens a lion that agrees to spare his life in return for a future favor.

Preparation Before the Puppet Show

• Locate or create the puppets.
• Read through your favorite version of the fable several times to familiarize yourself with the tale or memorize the script below.

Before the Presentation

• Place the mouse puppet on your right hand and the lion puppet on your left hand (vice versa for lefties).

Presentation

Narrator:
One day the King of the Jungle, a big, ferocious lion, decided to take a nap.

(Raise the lion puppet up for the audience to see and then have him lie down or rest in your lap.)

Narrator:
A mouse was out walking.

(As you move the mouse puppet toward the lion, have the mouse pause and look at the audience. Then have the mouse puppet climb on the lion and speak in a tiny voice.)

Mouse:
Oh, King of the Jungle, are you taking a nap?

(The lion puppet awakes with a jerk.)

Lion:
Roar! Not any more!

Mouse:
Oh, King of the Jungle, I am so glad to meet you at last. I want you to be my friend.

(Raise the lion up and have him grab the mouse's tail or leg. The lion speaks in rough, gruff voice.)

Lion:
What is a tiny little mouse doing waking me from my nap?
I'm going to eat you for my afternoon snack!

(The lion starts to chomp on the mouse's head. The mouse says in a frightened voice.)

Mouse:
Wait! Wait! Please, King of the Jungle. I'm sorry I disturbed you.
Please spare my life and do not eat me and one day I will return the favor to you!

Lion:
Roar! I'd like to know what kind of favor an itty, bitty mouse could ever
do for a big, majestic lion, but I'm feeling generous today and will let you go.

Narrator:
Lion doubted that a tiny mouse would ever be able to do him a favor,
but decided to release the mouse anyway.

(Have the mouse scamper behind your back.)

Narrator:
About a month later, the King of the Jungle was searching through the jungle,
quietly stalking for something to eat, and he walked under a big tree.

*(The lion moves away, stalking animals. Move the lion slowly from one side of stage
area to another, looking from left to right as if he is searching for prey.)*

Narrator:
Suddenly, a net dropped from the tree. A BIG net. It trapped him and he couldn't move.

*(If using a net or a rope, throw it over the lion or simply simulate this action. Suddenly,
flop the lion over as if caught. The lion roars loudly several times.)*

Lion:
Roar! Roar! Roar!

Narrator:
He jerked and he jerked and tried to get his teeth around bits of the net,
but nothing would do. He thought, What am I going to do?

(Wiggle the lion to show him struggling to free himself.)

Narrator:
And who do you think came along about then? The mouse!

(Bring the mouse out from behind your back and have him scamper toward the lion.)

Mouse:
Oh, King of the Jungle! How awful to be caught in a net! I remember the
day you spared my life, and now I am here to return the favor!

(The lion roars piteously.)

Lion:
Roar! Can you get someone to help me?

Mouse (says, boldly):
I don't know anyone who can help, but I can!

Narrator:
The mouse chewed on the net and freed the lion.

(Move the mouse over the lion. If the mouse puppet has a moveable mouth open and close it to show that he is chewing. If only the arms of the mouse move, use them to mime the actions of pulling and tugging at the net. The lion jumps up and shakes himself all over to show that he is free.)

Lion:
Thank you, mouse, thank you! You have saved my life. You are a true friend!

(Have the puppets hug and move off together now, forever friends.)

Narrator:
And that is the story of "The Lion and the Mouse." What is the moral of the fable? What did you learn?

(The audience might say something like "Kindness is more important than strength." Accept any reasonable answers from the audience.)

Variations

- An online collection of Aesop's fables is available at http://www.aesopfables.com/.
- This classic fable is available in most collections of Aesop's, including these:

  - Morpurgo, Michael. *The McElderry Book of Aesop's Fables*. New York: Simon & Schuster Children's Publishing Division, 2004.
  - Pinkney, Jerry. *Aesop's Fables*. San Francisco: Chronicle Books, 2000.

Lion Puppet

Materials

Two pieces of 9-inch by 12-inch gold felt

Scrap of black felt for nose

Scrap of yellow felt for lion's mane

Black embroidery thread for whiskers

Two wiggle eyes

Scissors

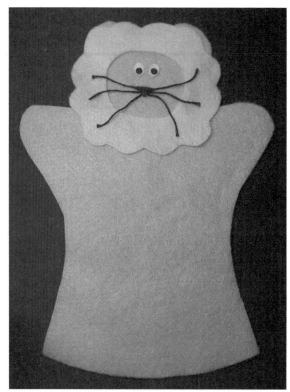

Figure 5-30   Felt Lion Puppet

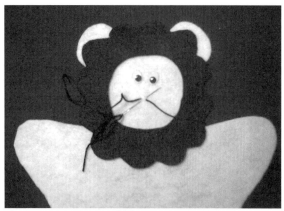

Figure 5-31   Lion's Whiskers

Glue

Needle

Directions

THE BODY

1. Photocopy or trace the patterns in the "Puppet Patterns Pantry" on pages 145–146 for the body of the lion and the mane. Cut out the patterns.
2. Cut the body of the lion puppet from the gold felt.
3. Cut the mane from the yellow felt.
4. Glue the mane around the face of the puppet.
5. Glue two wiggle eyes on the face of the lion.
6. Draw three strands of embroidery thread through the center of the face for the whiskers. (See Figure 5-31.)
7. Cut out a small black triangle for the lion's nose.
8. Glue the nose in the center of the whiskers.

9. Glue the two pieces of the gold felt together. Leave the bottom of the puppet open to put your hand through.

10. Set the puppet aside for the glue to dry.

Mouse Puppet

Materials

Two pieces of 9-inch by 12-inch gray felt for mouse

Scrap of pink felt for inside of mouse's ears

Scrap of black felt for nose

Black embroidery thread for whiskers

Two wiggle eyes

Scissors

Glue

Needle

Figure 5-32   Felt Mouse Puppet

The Body

1. Photocopy or trace the patterns in the "Puppet Patterns Pantry" on pages 145–146 to create the body of the mouse and the ears. Cut out the patterns.

2. Cut out the body of the puppet from the gray felt.

3. Cut out two inner ears from a scrap of pink felt.

4. Glue the inner ears onto the ears on the body of the puppet.

5. Glue two wiggle eyes on the face of the mouse.

6. Draw three strands of embroidery thread through the center of the face for the whiskers. (See Figure 5-33.)

7. Cut out a small black triangle for the mouse's nose.

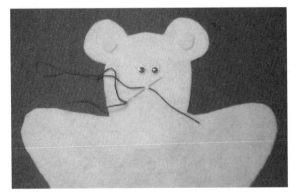

Figure 5-33   Mouse's Whiskers

8. Glue the nose in the center of the whiskers.

9. Glue the two pieces of the gray felt together. Leave the bottom of the puppet open for you to stick your hand through.

10. Set the puppet aside for the glue to dry.

The Tortoise and the Hare

Fable

Ages 6 to 12
Time: 5 minutes

Puppets Needed

One tortoise
One hare

Purchasing Puppets Tips

Tortoise and hare puppets are easy to find, and these animals frequently appear in stories, so consider purchasing well-constructed puppets, because you will find lots of uses for these two characters as you develop your puppet storytelling. When purchasing a tortoise puppet you might want to look for one in which the head, tail, and legs can retract into the shell completely. Whereas that feature is not needed for this presentation, when you finish the story you can demonstrate for the audience how turtles draw into their shells to protect themselves from harm. Look for a hare puppet that allows you to put your hand in through the very end of the puppet near the tail. This allows you to manipulate the feet and the head of the puppet to make its hopping and sniffing actions more realistic.

The Story

A speedy hare challenges a slow-moving tortoise to a race.

Preparation Before the Puppet Show

- Locate or create the puppets.
- Read through your favorite version of the fable several times to familiarize yourself with the tale or memorize the script below.

Before the Presentation

- Place the tortoise puppet on your left hand and the hare puppet on your right hand (vice versa for lefties).

Presentation

Narrator:
This is the story of the tortoise and the hare. It doesn't matter whether you call the tortoise a tortoise, a turtle, or even a Tortuga, and it doesn't matter whether you call the hare a hare, a rabbit, a bunny, or a jackrabbit—the story is still the same. Once upon a time, at the edge of the forest near the river, there lived a tortoise.

(Have the tortoise puppet look at the audience and make eye contact.)

Narrator:
And a hare.

(Have the hare puppet look at the audience and make eye contact.)

Narrator:
Now, the tortoise was very, very slow.

(Move the tortoise forward very, very slowly.)

Narrator:
And the hare was very, very fast.

(Have the hare rush from left to right and from right to left in front of you very fast.)

Narrator:
The hare got very, very bored, and one day he said to the tortoise,

(Have the hare speak very fast, just like he runs.)

Hare:
Tortoise, I'm bored. Let's have a race. You and me. We'll race to
the river and whoever gets there first wins.

*(Have the hare and the tortoise look at each other as they talk.
Speak very, very slowly for the tortoise.)*

Tortoise:
Well, Hare, it doesn't seem like much of a race to me.
I'm kind of slow and you're kind of fast.

Hare:
That doesn't really matter; I just like to win. So let's have a race.
Let's ask Fox to give us a start.

Narrator:
So they went to Fox.

(No fox puppet is needed, because he has only two lines and is offstage.)

Hare:
Fox, would you be our starter?

Narrator:
Fox agreed to be the starter.

(Bring the hare puppet up in front of your chest and move the tortoise
puppet alongside him. Both puppets should face the audience.)

Fox:
Get ready, get set, GO!

Narrator:
Off went the hare whisking away, trotting along, and then came the tortoise.
Hare kept going and going as fast as he could.

(Quickly stretch your arm with the hare out in front of you and slip
the tortoise puppet behind you so that it is unseen by the audience.
Turn the hare to look back toward you.)

Narrator:
He turned around and looked and didn't see Tortoise.

Hare:
I knew that Tortoise couldn't keep up with me! I can't even see him way back there. I might
as well take a little nap while he tries to catch up with me. If he ever catches up,
I'll run on to the river and win the race!

Narrator:
So Hare folded himself up, put his ears to the ground, and took a nap.

(Place the hare in your lap to take his nap. Slowly bring the tortoise
puppet from behind your back. Have him glance down at the
sleeping hare as he passes him.)

Tortoise:
Look at Hare taking a nap. My goodness! Hare is sound asleep.
He must be really tired. I'll try not to wake him up.

Narrator:
So Tortoise kept going on to the river.

(Slip the tortoise puppet behind you so that it is unseen by the audience.)

Narrator:
In a little while, Hare woke up and yawned and stretched.

(Wake up the hare and have him look around at the audience as he searches for the tortoise.)

Hare:
Hmm. Still no Tortoise. He must be really far back.
I guess I'll go on to the river, our finish line.

(The hare strolls nonchalantly toward the imaginary river/finish line. Bring the tortoise out from behind your back and place him in front of the hare.)

Narrator:
But just as Hare got to the river, there was Tortoise, and there was Fox saying . . .

Fox:
And the winner is the tortoise!

Narrator:
Hare was so upset he jumped up and down.

(Move the hare puppet up and down angrily.)

Hare:
Wait! Wait! This isn't possible! This was rigged!
I'm much faster than Tortoise! He could not have won.
What in the world is going on here?

Tortoise:
Well, Hare, I saw you earlier taking a nap and decided the
polite thing to do was let you sleep!

(Have the tortoise look at the audience.)

Tortoise:
You know, there is a moral to this story. A moral is a sentence that
tells us something we should learn from the story. What is the moral of
the fable? What did you learn?

*(The audience might say something like "Slow and steady wins the race."
Accept any reasonable answers from the audience.)*

Variations

- An online collection of Aesop's fables is available at http://www.aesopfables.com/.
- This classic fable is available in most collections of Aesop's, including these:

• Morpurgo, Michael. *The McElderry Book of Aesop's Fables*. New York: Simon & Schuster Children's Publishing Division, 2004.
• Pinkney, Jerry. *Aesop's Fables*. San Francisco: Chronicle Books, 2000.

The Tortoise

Materials

Three paper plates

Two small wiggle eyes

Glue and glue gun or stapler and staples

Scissors

Green paint

Paintbrush

Thin black marker

Figure 5-34   Tortoise Paper Plate Puppet

Directions

1. Paint three paper plates green. One will be the top shell of the tortoise, one will be the bottom shell of the tortoise, and the third will be used to make the tortoise's head, feet, and tail.
2. Follow the directions for the paper plate puppet in Chapter 3 on pages 27–30.
3. Cut the four feet from the rim of the third paper plate. Each foot should be 1½ inches long. (See Figure 5-35.)
4. Cut a ¾-inch section from rim of the third paper plate for the tortoise's tail.

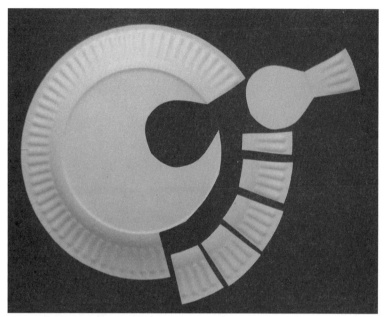

Figure 5-35   Tortoise's Head, Legs, and Tail

5. Cut a circular shape with a neck from the bottom of the paper plate for the tortoise's head. (See Figure 5-35.)
6. Glue two small wiggle eyes on the head of the tortoise.
7. Draw on his mouth with a thin marker.
8. Staple or glue the head, legs, and tail to the top side of one of the paper plates. (See Figure 5-36.)
9. Staple or glue the two plates together, leaving an opening by the tail large enough to slip your hand inside.

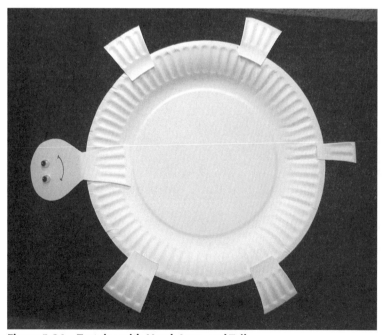

Figure 5-36   Tortoise with Head, Legs, and Tail

Hare

Figure 5-37   Hare Paper Plate Puppet

Materials

Two paper plates

Two sheets of white construction paper or photocopy paper

Two chenille sticks

Two large wiggle eyes

One pompom

Glue gun and glue or stapler and staples

Scissors

Directions

1. Follow the directions for the basic paper plate puppet in Chapter 3 on pages 27–30.
2. Photocopy or trace the pattern for the hare's ears in the "Puppet Patterns Pantry" on page 147.
3. Cut the ears out of white paper.
4. Make a slight fold at the bottom of the ears to give them some depth.
5. Glue the ears and legs to the rim of the top side of a paper plate. See Figure 5-38 to guide you in the placement.
6. Glue a second paper plate on top. Leave an opening at the bottom large enough to slip your hand inside.

Figure 5-38   Hare's Ears and Legs

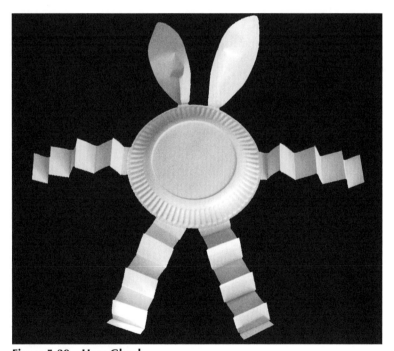

Figure 5-39   Hare Glued

7. Glue the wiggle eyes in the top third of the paper plate.
8. Glue the chenille stick whiskers in the center of the paper plate.
9. Glue the pompom on top of the whiskers right in the center of them.

6

MEETING TWENTIETH-CENTURY FRIENDS

KITTEN'S FIRST FULL MOON

Henkes, Kevin. *Kitten's First Full Moon.* New York: Greenwillow Books/HarperCollins, 2004.

Picture Book

Ages 3 to 8
Time: 3 to 5 minutes

Puppet Needed

One kitten puppet

Figure 6-1　Kitten

Props Needed

One large bowl

The Story

A very young kitten sees her very first full moon and decides that the moon is a bowl of milk just for her. Stretching her neck, jumping from the porch, running toward it, and climbing up a tree do not get her any closer to the bowl of milk. When all her attempts fail, she returns home exhausted, wet, and famished to discover that on the porch is a delicious bowl of creamy milk.

Preparation Before the Puppet Show

- Locate or create a kitten puppet.
- Locate a large bowl.
- Read the story several times and create a list of Kitten's actions, including:

    1. Stretches, licks, and catches a bug;
    2. Wiggles, jumps, and falls down;
    3. Chases it and does not get any closer;
    4. Climbs the tree and still cannot reach it;
    5. Jumps from the tree and gets wet; and
    6. Goes home and finds a bowl of milk on the porch.

- If you are using a realistic kitten puppet, spend some time studying the movements of a real kitten and practice re-creating the kitten's movements with your puppet.

Before the Presentation

- Place the kitten puppet on your left hand so you can use your right hand to pick up the bowl (vice versa for lefties).
- Place the bowl behind you within easy reach but out of sight of the audience.

Presentation

Have the kitten puppet scan the audience making eye contact as you state the title of the book and the author. Speak slowly and articulate clearly so that your audience can understand you. Because there is no dialogue in the story, you can use your natural speaking voice for the narration. Whenever the narration calls the kitten "Poor Kitten," speak in a very sorrowful voice.

After Kitten spies the bowl of milk in the sky, she makes several unsuccessful attempts to get to the milk. You might find it helpful to keep a short list of Kitten's actions nearby as you perform. As you describe each action, have the puppet act them out.

Stretches, licks, and catches a bug.

(With your free hand stretch out the puppet's front legs and then open and close the puppet's mouth if it is moveable.)

Wiggles, jumps, and falls down.

(Move the puppet from side to side, then up and down to simulate jump. Flop the puppet over on its back on your lap.)

Chases it and does not get any closer.

(Move the puppet quickly back and forth in front of the audience.)

Climbs the tree and still cannot reach it.

(Slowly stretch out your arm, moving the puppet upward.)

Jumps from the tree and gets wet.

(Quickly drop your arm as the kitten jumps from the tree. Then, shake the puppet back and forth as though shaking off the water.)

Goes home and finds a bowl of milk on the porch.

(Reach for the bowl beside you and place it in front of you as you move the puppet toward the bowl. Nod the puppet's head up and down to simulate drinking the milk in the bowl.)

Kitten Puppet

Figure 6-2   Kitten Paper Plate Puppet

Follow the directions in Chapter 3 on pages 27–30 for a kitten paper plate puppet.

Figure 6-3   Rabbit

THE TALE OF PETER RABBIT

Potter, Beatrix. *The Tale of Peter Rabbit.* New York: Penguin, 2002.

Picture Book

Ages 4 to 10
Time: 10 minutes

Puppet Needed

One rabbit puppet

Props Needed

One coat for the rabbit puppet (optional)
One watering can (optional)

The Story

Four little bunnies, dressed in their finery, are told by Mother Rabbit to stay away from Mr. McGregor's garden. While his siblings obey and pick blackberries and return home in their fine clothes, Peter disobeys, and is almost caught by Mr. McGregor. He loses his coat, has a series of frightening adventures including being trapped inside a watering can, and returns home with a bad cold. His brother and sisters have blackberries and milk for dinner, but all Peter gets is chamomile tea for his cold.

Preparation Before the Puppet Show

- Locate or create a rabbit puppet.
- Locate the props.
- Learn the story.

Before the Presentation

- Place the rabbit puppet on your left hand so you can use your right hand to pick up the props (vice versa for lefties).
- Place the watering can beside you within easy reach.

Presentation

Introduce the story by having Peter Rabbit make eye contact with your audience as you state the name of the story and the author of the story. Using a kind, motherly voice, have Mother Bunny give instructions to the bunny children, telling them to take care of the new coats she has made for each of them. She reminds the children to stay away from Mr. McGregor's garden.

Peter immediately heads for Mr. McGregor's garden.

(Quickly move Peter from the right to left side as you describe him running to Mr. McGregor's garden.)

List the different vegetables that Peter is nibbling—lettuces, French beans, radishes, and parsley.

(Dip the puppet up and down to simulate him eating the vegetables. Suddenly have the puppet stop moving when spotted by Mr. McGregor. Then, shake the puppet nervously.)

Have Peter run, get caught in a net, and then fall down.

(Move the puppet quickly from your right to your left in front of you. Stop the puppet and drop him into your lap wiggling.)

Tell the audience how Peter gets out of the net by slipping out of his new coat.

(If your puppet has a removable coat, take it off and dangle it as though caught in a net. Then, place the coat beside you.)

Peter runs until he sees a large watering can.

(If you have a large enough watering can, put the puppet inside the watering can; otherwise, just tell the audience that he hides in the watering can.)

Tell how Mr. McGregor gives up looking for Peter and goes home.

(Take the puppet out of the watering can or simply describe how he climbs out of the watering can. Move the puppet quickly as though he is running toward home. Using a motherly voice, have Mother Bunny scold Peter because he is wet and has lost his new coat.)

Mother gives Peter a cup of hot chamomile tea and puts him to bed. From his bed he can see his siblings eating milk and blackberries.

(Hold up Peter's coat and tell the audience how Mr. McGregor put Peter's coat on his scarecrow. Ask your audience what they think about Peter's behavior and what they think he learned from his experiences.)

Figure 6-4   Felt Peter Rabbit Puppet

Rabbit Puppet

Materials

Three pieces of 9-inch by 12-inch brown felt

One piece of 9-inch by 12-inch blue felt

Scrap of pink felt for inside of rabbit's ears and rabbit's nose

Black embroidery thread for whiskers

Two wiggle eyes

Two small flat buttons

Scissors

Glue

Needle

Directions

THE BODY

1. Photocopy or trace the patterns in the "Puppet Patterns Pantry" on pages 129–130 and page 148 for the basic felt hand puppet, the rabbit's inner ears, and the rabbit's outer ears. Cut out the patterns.
2. Follow the directions in Chapter 3 on pages 25–26 for the basic felt hand puppet.
3. Cut two bodies from the basic felt hand puppet pattern using the brown felt.
4. Cut two outer ears from the brown felt.
5. Cut two inner ears from the scrap of pink felt.
6. Glue the inner ears on top of the outer ears. (See Figure 6-5.)
7. Thread a needle with three strands of embroidery thread.

Figure 6-5   Peter Rabbit's Ears

8. Draw three strands of embroidery thread through the center of the face for the whiskers. See Figure 5-31 on page 86.
9. Cut a small pink triangle for the rabbit's nose.
10. Glue the nose in the center of the whiskers.
11. Glue two wiggle eyes on the face of the rabbit just above the whiskers.
12. Glue or stitch together the two pieces of the body. Leave the bottom of the puppet open for you to put your hand through.

THE COAT

1. Photocopy or trace the pattern in the "Puppet Patterns Pantry" on page 149 for Peter Rabbit's coat. Cut out the pattern.
2. Cut two coats of the blue felt.
3. Fold one piece in half down the center and cut through the fold to form the opening for the coat.
4. Glue the shoulders of the coat and the sides of the coat.
5. Leave the neck open, the sleeve ends open, and the bottom of the coat open.
6. Glue two small buttons on the left center front of the coat. See Figure 6-7 to determine the placement of the buttons.
7. Let the glue dry.
8. Slip the coat on the puppet.

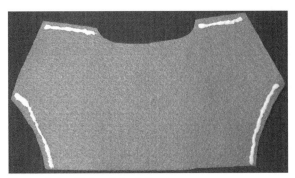

Figure 6-6   Gluing Peter's Coat

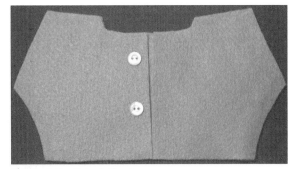

Figure 6-7   Peter's Coat

STELLALUNA

Cannon, Janell. *Stellaluna*. San Diego: Harcourt, 1993.

Picture Book

Ages 5 to 10
Time: 10 minutes

Purchasing Puppets Tips

There are Stellaluna puppets available in different sizes, and some of them are sold with copies of the book. Bat puppets are available from various suppliers, and you are sure to find one in your price range. While there are several bats and birds in the story, only one bat puppet is required for this presentation.

Puppet Needed

One bat puppet

Figure 6-8 Bat

The Story

While searching for food one night, an owl attacks Mother Bat and her tiny baby bat, Stellaluna, falls from the sky into a bird's nest. The three baby birds in the nest and their mother adopt Stellaluna. Mother Bird teaches Stellaluna how to perch on limbs instead of hanging from them, how to eat insects instead of fruit, and how to sleep at night and fly during the day instead of sleeping during the day and flying at night. Stellaluna tries very hard to act like a bird, but she is a bat, and it is difficult for her to act like a bird. One evening Stellaluna encounters a group of bats who are very amused at her birdlike behaviors. Stellaluna and her mother are reunited. Now, Stellaluna can revert to her bat ways.

Preparation Before the Puppet Show

- Locate a Stellaluna puppet or create a bat puppet.
- Read through the story several times to become familiar with the order of the events and to become familiar with the dialogue.
- You might find it helpful to create an outline of the events in the story similar to the one below.

1. Stellaluna and mother fly out to search for food.
2. Owl attacks.
3. Stellaluna lands in a bird's nest.
4. Stellaluna hangs by her feet from the bird's nest.
5. Stellaluna eats a grasshopper.
6. Stellaluna learns to stay awake during the day and sleep at night.
7. Stellaluna teaches the baby birds to hang from their nest by their feet.
8. Stellaluna upsets Mother Bird.
9. Stellaluna agrees not to hang by her feet anymore.
10. Stellaluna behaves like a good bird should.
11. Stellaluna and the baby birds fly from the nest.
12. Stellaluna gets separated from the baby birds.
13. Stellaluna is reunited with Mother Bat and begins acting like a bat—eating fruit, hanging by her feet, flying at night.
14. Stellaluna visits the birds and takes them flying at night.
15. Stellaluna and the birds wonder how they can be so alike and yet so different.

Before the Presentation

- Place the bat puppet on your right hand (vice versa for lefties).

Presentation

Even though there are several different characters in this story, you only need one puppet, a bat. As you tell the story, use different voices for the different characters. Use a kind, mature voice for Mother Bat, a childlike, tiny voice for Stellaluna, a cross voice for Mother Bird, and childlike voices for the little birds. The different expressions you use in the voices make this story a charmer for young children. Because there are four different voices in this presentation, you will want to practice to make sure you maintain the same voice for the characters throughout the presentation. The different voices are important because you will be using only one puppet and the voices identify who is speaking.

As you begin the story, state the title and the name of the author as Stellaluna establishes eye contact with the audience. You might find it helpful to have your outline of the story nearby as you perform.

Stellaluna and Mother Bat fly out to search for food.

(Hold the puppet high above your head and have it dip and twirl as it flies through the air.)

Owl attacks.

(Drop the puppet while it is high in the air.)

Stellaluna lands in a bird's nest.

(Catch the puppet as it falls.)

Stellaluna hangs by her feet from the bird's nest.

(Hold the puppet upside down by its feet. Use three distinctive (and different) voices for the three little birds that comment on the newcomer hanging upside down from their nest.)

Stellaluna eats a grasshopper.

(If your puppet has a moveable mouth, open and close the mouth. If not, just describe the action and make a yucky face as Stellaluna swallows the grasshopper.)

Stellaluna learns to stay awake during the day and sleep at night.

(Hold the puppet still and have it make eye contact with the audience by turning from side to side.)

Stellaluna teaches the baby birds to hang from their nest by their feet.

(Hold the puppet upside down by its feet.)

Stellaluna upsets Mother Bird.

(Use a cross voice for Mother Bird as she scolds Stellaluna.)

Stellaluna agrees not to hang by her feet anymore.

(Use a contrite voice for Stellaluna as she agrees to Mother Bird's wishes.)

Stellaluna behaves like a good bird should.

(Hold the puppet still and have it make eye contact with the audience by turning from side to side.)

Stellaluna and the baby birds fly from the nest.

(Hold the puppet high above your head and have it dip and twirl as it flies through the air.)

Stellaluna gets separated from the baby birds.

(Move the puppet to your far right.)

Stellaluna is reunited with Mother Bat and begins acting like a bat—eating fruit, hanging by her feet, flying at night.

(Hold the puppet still and have it face the audience. Use a very excited voice when Mother Bat realizes that this is her Stellaluna. If your audience is getting restless you may want to end the presentation here.)

Stellaluna visits the birds and takes them flying at night.

(Hold the puppet high above your head and have it dip and twirl as it flies through the air.)

Stellaluna and the birds wonder how they can be so alike and yet so different.

(Conclude the presentation by having Stellaluna look at the audience as she and the baby birds talk about how they are different but also the same.)

Bat Puppet

Figure 6-9   Bat Felt Puppet

Materials

Two pieces of 9-inch by 12-inch brown felt

Two wiggle eyes

Glue

Scissors

Directions

1. Photocopy or trace the pattern in the "Puppet Patterns Pantry" on page 150 for the bat puppet head and wings. Cut out the pattern.
2. Cut the bat puppet head and wings out of brown felt.
3. Cut a 6-inch by 9-inch rectangle of brown felt for the puppet body.
4. Roll the brown felt rectangle up in a tube starting on the 6-inch side.

5. Overlap the sides by about ½ inch.
6. Glue the tube together.
7. Squirt a bead of glue on one end of the open tube. Leave the other end of the tube open for you to insert your hand on the finished puppet.
8. Pinch the end of the tube together. Hold the end closed for a few seconds for the glue to dry.
9. Glue the closed end of the tube just under the bat head on top of the bat wings with the seam side down. (See Figure 6-9.)
10. Put a dot of glue at the other end of the tube to anchor the body to the wings.
11. Leave this end of the tube open for you to insert your hand.
12. Glue the wiggle eyes on the bat head using the photograph in Figure 6-9 to determine the exact placement.
13. Set the puppet aside for the glue to dry.

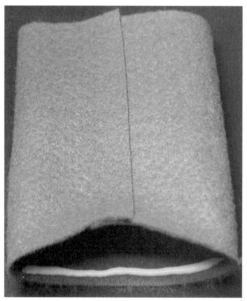

Figure 6-10   Glue on End of Tube

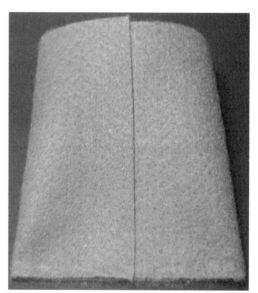

Figure 6-11   Sealed Tube

SYLVESTER AND THE MAGIC PEBBLE

Steig, William. *Sylvester and the Magic Pebble.* New York: Simon & Schuster Books for Young Readers, 1969.

Picture Book

Ages 4 to 10.

Time: 10 minutes

Puppet Needed

One donkey puppet

Props Needed

One red pebble

The Story

One day Sylvester finds a beautiful, shiny, red, round pebble. He discovers that when he holds the pebble his wishes come true and that is when his troubles begin. Frightened by a lion, he wishes he is a rock and he becomes one. But a rock cannot hold a pebble to make wishes and so Sylvester is doomed to remain a rock. Sylvester's parents search for him but cannot find him. One day his parents discover the red pebble and place it on the rock as they reminisce about their son. Sylvester wishes he were once again a donkey and he becomes one. Now, the family has everything they ever wanted—each other.

Figure 6-12   Donkey Puppet

Preparation Before the Puppet Show

- Locate or construct a donkey puppet.
- Locate a red pebble or spray paint a brown pebble red.
- Read through the story several times to become familiar with the order of the events in the story and to become familiar with the dialogue. Decide which if any parts of the story you will leave out. For example, you may decide to leave out the part about the police and the dogs looking for Sylvester.
- You might find it helpful to create an outline of the events in the story similar to the one below.

  1. Sylvester states his name, that he lives with his parents, and that he collects unusual pebbles.
  2. Sylvester finds a magic pebble that grants his wishes when he is holding it.

3. Sylvester stops and starts the rain by wishing.
4. Sylvester encounters a lion, panics, wishes he were a rock, and becomes a rock.
5. Sylvester cannot turn himself back into a donkey because he is no longer holding the magic pebble.
6. His parents look for him.
7. Parents picnic on the rock.
8. Father picks up the magic pebble and places it on the rock.
9. Sylvester wishes he were a donkey again.
10. His wish is granted and he is reunited with his parents.

Before the Presentation

- Place the donkey puppet on your right hand (vice versa for lefties).
- Conceal the red pebble in your other hand.

Presentation

Have Sylvester scan the audience to make eye contact. State the title of the book and the author.

(Use a childlike voice for Sylvester.)

Have Sylvester state his name, that he lives with his parents, and that he collects unusual pebbles. Tell how he finds a magic pebble that grants his wishes when he is holding it.

(Reveal the red pebble in your hand and hold it up for the audience to see. Have Sylvester discover it and exclaim how unusual it is. If your puppet is not capable of holding the pebble, place it near his hoof. While it might be tempting to have the puppet hold the pebble in his mouth, this is not something you want to model for young children.)

He stops and starts the rain by wishing.

(When it stops raining, have the puppet look up at the sky. Repeat this sequence when he tries the wish again, so that the audience understands the magic works only when Sylvester is holding the pebble.)

Then, he encounters a lion, panics, wishes he were a rock, and becomes a rock.

(When the lion approaches, Sylvester should be holding the pebble as he wishes and becomes a rock. When he becomes a rock, place the puppet behind you so that he is removed from sight. Close your hand to conceal the pebble.)

Sylvester cannot turn himself back into a donkey because he is no longer holding the magic pebble. His parents look for him.

*(When the parents, who speak in sad but mature voices, commiserate over
Sylvester's disappearance, no puppets are necessary. Simply tell the audience
how they looked for their son.)*

Parents picnic on the rock.
Father picks up the magic pebble, places it on the rock, and says it reminds him of his son.

(Open your hand to reveal the pebble and hold it up for the audience to see.)

Sylvester wishes he could be a donkey again.

*(Bring the puppet out from behind your back. You may need to practice retrieving the puppet from
behind you in order to get Sylvester to suddenly appear.)*

His wish is granted and he is reunited with his parents.

*(The puppet should be very animated at this point to show his excitement about being
reunited with his parents.)*

Conclude by saying, "And that's the story of Sylvester and the Magic Pebble."

Donkey Puppet

Materials

Three pieces of 9-inch by 12-inch dark brown felt

Scraps of light brown felt and black felt

Two wiggle eyes (optional)

Scissors

Glue

Directions

1. Photocopy or trace the patterns in the "Puppet Patterns Pantry" on pages 129 and 151 for the basic felt hand puppet and for the donkey head. Cut out the patterns.
2. Follow the directions in Chapter 3 on pages 25–26 for a felt hand puppet.
3. Cut out two bodies from the dark brown felt.
4. Cut two heads from the dark brown felt.
5. Cut two inner ears from the light brown felt.
6. Cut two small circles for the donkey's nostrils from the black felt.

Figure 6-13   Felt Donkey Puppet

Figure 6-14   Donkey Head

7. Glue the wiggle eyes, inner ears, and nostrils on one of the faces. (See Figure 6-14.)
8. Glue the donkey heads to the body pieces.
9. Glue the two pieces of felt together or stitch them together. Leave the bottom of the puppet open for you to stick your hand through.
10. Set the puppet aside for the glue to dry.

VERDI

Cannon, Janell. *Verdi*. San Diego: Harcourt Brace, 1997.

Picture Book

Ages 4 to 10

Time: 20 minutes

Purchasing Puppets Tips

In the story Verdi is a small yellow tree python that turns into a green tree python as he matures. There are a Verdi hand puppet and finger puppet available from some online booksellers. If you cannot find a Verdi hand puppet, use a small yellow snake puppet to begin your presentation and end it with a large green snake puppet. Verdi is also available as a plush animal that you can hold as you tell the story. If you have a fish puppet, you can incorporate it into the story, but it is not essential.

Puppets Needed

One Python puppet or

One small yellow snake and

One large green snake

One fish puppet (optional)

The Story

Figure 6-15   Python Puppet

Verdi, a small yellow python, does not want to grow up, lose his yellow coloring, and become sedentary like the adult pythons. His lively, daring adventures, including flinging himself into the air in an attempt to reach the sun, leave him injured. While being cared for by some adult pythons, he discovers that they had once been adventurous just like him. To his dismay, he matures and turns green. However, when approached by some young pythons, Verdi's adventurous spirit returns and he decides to show them how to safely launch themselves into the air.

Preparation Before the Puppet Show

- Locate or construct a snake puppet.
- Read through the story several times to become familiar with the order of the events in the story and to become familiar with the dialogue.
- You might find it helpful to create an outline of the events in the story similar to the one below.

   1. Verdi does not want to grow up.
   2. Verdi meets three older pythons.
   3. Verdi soars toward the sun.
   4. Verdi is rescued by older pythons.
   5. Verdi meets young pythons.

- In addition to Verdi, there are three mature pythons, Umbles, Aggie, and Ribbon, and each needs a different distinctive voice. It will take practice to keep all of the voices separate. Tape record your performance. As you play it back, listen to determine if you can tell the voices apart and if you used the correct voice for each snake throughout your presentation.

Before the Presentation

- Begin the presentation with the snake in a natural position such as draped over your shoulder or wrapped around your arm. You will need both hands to depict all of Verdi's escapades as he rebels against the idea of turning green and growing boring and rude.
- If you are using a green snake puppet and/or a fish puppet, put these puppets beside you within easy reach.

Presentation

The story begins when Verdi's mother urges her little yellow hatchlings out into the world to become adult snakes and turn green like the leaves on the trees. Verdi likes his bright yellow color and wonders why he should want to be big and green.

(Have Verdi scan the audience to make eye contact as he states the title and the author of the story. Move the snake from one side to the other so the audience can see him.)

He looks in the treetops and finds some older snakes to query.

(At this point in the story, have your snake puppet address his questions to the audience

as if they were the older snakes. Umbles, Aggie, and Ribbon respond to Verdi rather rudely and seem lazy and bored.)

Verdi soars toward the sun.

(Raise him up as high as you can to show him launching himself into the air. While the puppet is aloft, have the older snakes mutter to each other that he probably will not live to turn green. If you have both a yellow and a green snake, switch to the green snake at this time.)

However, to Verdi's horror, he does live to turn green.

(If your snake has a mouth that opens, open it wide to show Verdi's horror.)

He snatches some leaves with his mouth and uses them to try to rub off the green.

(Move the snake's mouth up and down his body to show him trying to rub off the green color.)

Verdi decides to wash off the green in the river.

(Drop your hand downward to indicate him diving into the river. If you have a fish puppet, place it on your other hand and have it lunge at the snake.)

Verdi bites the fish on the nose in his shock and fright.

(If you do not have a fish puppet, just mime the snake movements as you narrate what is happening.)

When Verdi slithers away, he becomes covered with mud, which hardens and dries.

(As you narrate this part of the adventure, hold the puppet very still and stiff. As the mud breaks off, slowly wiggle the puppet.)

Tell how Verdi decides that the bright yellow sun in the sky will make him yellow again.

(Point the snake's head up toward the sky. To show him launching himself to the sun, have the snake start from near the ground and soar as far as you can reach. Then, have him fall back to earth and bow his head in misery.)

To show the old snakes rescuing Verdi, stretch the snake down the length of your arm.

(Hold him very still with his eyes focusing on the audience as he listens to the old snakes talk about all the adventures they had when they were young like Verdi.)

When Verdi heals he is approached by two young hatchlings.

(Quickly snap his head upward and slowly turn his head so that he can make eye contact with the audience members.)

Describe how Verdi teaches the hatchlings to launch themselves safely so they can make figure eights in the air.

(Raise Verdi high in the air so that he can soar.)

At the end of the presentation have the snake take a bow and say, "And that's the story of Verdi."

Snake Puppets

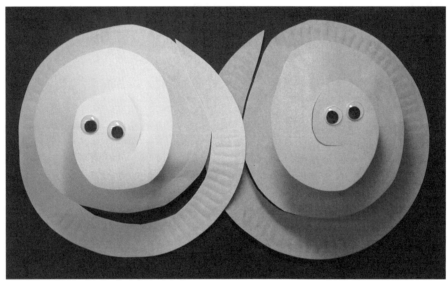

Figure 6-16   Snake Paper Plate Puppets

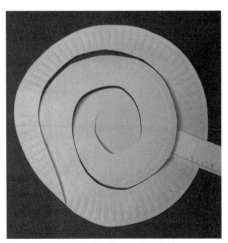

Figure 6-17   Snake Puppet Spirals

Materials

Two white paper plates

Green and yellow acrylic craft paint

One 2-inch paintbrush or foam brush

Four wiggle eyes

Scissors

Directions

1. Paint one paper plate green and paint one yellow. Paint both sides of the plates.
2. Set the paper plates aside to dry.
3. Cut the paper plates into spirals starting on the outside edge and ending in the center with an oval or circle

for the snake's head. The spirals should be about 1¼ inches to 1½ inches wide. (See Figure 6-17.)

4. Glue two wiggle eyes on the snakeheads. See Figure 6-16 for the placement of the wiggle eyes.
5. Set the snakes aside for the glue to dry.

THE VERY HUNGRY CATERPILLAR

Carle, Eric. *The Very Hungry Caterpillar.* New York: Philomel Books, 1969.

Picture Book

Ages 3 to 10
Time: 10 minutes

Puppets Needed

One caterpillar puppet
One butterfly puppet

Figure 6-18   Caterpillar and Butterfly

Props Needed

One solid-color pillowcase
One white bean for the egg
One green leaf
One apple
Two pears
Three plums
Four strawberries
Five oranges
Variety of junk food (optional)

The Story

One Sunday morning a very hungry caterpillar hatches from a tiny egg on a small leaf. He starts the week by eating his way through one apple. Each of the next five days he eats through two pears, three plums, four strawberries, and five oranges. The next day he eats a lot of junk food and ends up with a terrible stomachache. So, he eats a green leaf and begins to feel better. Now he is a very fat caterpillar and he spins a cocoon around himself. After a few weeks he nibbles a hole in the cocoon, pushes his way out, and emerges a beautiful butterfly.

Preparation Before the Puppet Show

- Locate or create a caterpillar puppet.
- Locate or create a butterfly puppet.
- Locate a pillowcase.
- Locate the fruit and junk food or create cutouts of the fruit.
- Locate a white bean.
- Read through the story several times to become familiar with the order of the events.

Before the Presentation

- Place the caterpillar puppet on your left hand so you can use your right hand to pick up the props. Keep the caterpillar behind your back as you introduce the story (vice versa for lefties).
- Place the white bean in your right hand (vice versa for lefties).
- Place the food in the correct order beside you or on a table in front of you.
- Place the butterfly in the pillowcase and put it to the side where you can easily reach for it.

Presentation

State the title of the story and the author.

(Hold the white bean up for the audience to see. As you tell about the caterpillar hatching from the egg, have the caterpillar pop up from behind your back. Point his eyes toward the audience so that he makes eye contact with the children.)

Tell the children that the hungry caterpillar began to look for food.

(As the caterpillar starts to look for some food, have the puppet look from side to side as if seeking something.)

Hold up the apple in front of the caterpillar's mouth.

(If you cannot put food in the puppet's mouth, simply hold up the props for the audience to see and then put the food back down.)

Repeat this for the two pears, the three plums, the four strawberries, the five oranges, and any other food you have included in your presentation.

(If you decide to include junk food in your presentation, tell the audience that the caterpillar was still hungry. You may want to simply describe the food rather than have it as props.)

After eating all that food, he got a stomachache.

(Turn the caterpillar over, belly up.)

He eats a green leaf and begins to feel better.

(Hold up the green leaf. Ask the children what their mothers give them when they have a stomachache, and they usually reply "Pepto Bismol" or "pink medicine." Then, explain that is why the caterpillar ate a green leaf.)

Now, the caterpillar was full and he was fat. So, he spun himself a cocoon or house where he stayed for two weeks.

(As you tell this part of the story, put your hand into the pillowcase and slip on the butterfly puppet. Slowly withdraw the butterfly.)

Fly the butterfly in front of your audience. Conclude by saying, "And that is the story of the Very Hungry Caterpillar."

Puppets

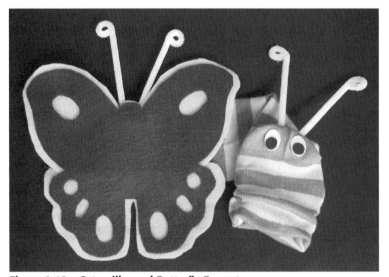

Figure 6-19   Caterpillar and Butterfly Puppets

Caterpillar

MATERIALS

One striped sock

Wiggle eyes

Thin cardboard for forming the mouth

One chenille stick for antennae

Pencil

Scissors

Glue

DIRECTIONS

1. Follow the directions for a basic sock puppet in Chapter 3 on pages 30–31.
2. Fold one chenille stick in half and wrap the ends around a pencil to curl them. (See Figure 6-20.)
3. Use a dab of hot glue to attach the antennae to the heel of the sock just behind the eyes. (See Figure 6-21.)

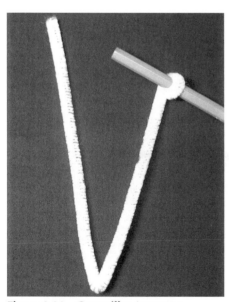

Figure 6-20   Caterpillar Antennae

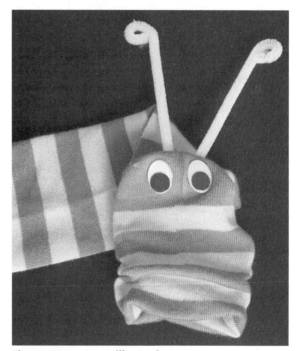

Figure 6-21   Caterpillar Sock Puppet

Butterfly

MATERIALS

Two pieces of 9-inch by 12-inch blue felt

One piece of 9-inch by 12-inch yellow felt

One piece of 9-inch by 12-inch pink felt

One chenille stick

Glue

Scissors

DIRECTIONS

1. Photocopy or trace the patterns in the "Puppet Patterns Pantry" on pages 152–154 for the butterfly puppet. Cut out the patterns.

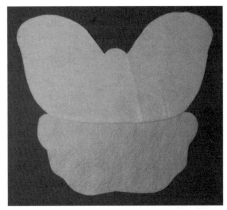

Figure 6-22   Butterfly Upper and Lower Bodies

2. Cut the upper body of the butterfly from pink felt and the lower body from yellow felt. When you glue the butterfly together, you will sandwich these two pieces between the two whole body pieces.

3. Cut two whole body pieces from light blue felt.

4. Glue the upper body to the lower body, overlapping them by about ⅛ of an inch. (See Figure 6-22.)

5. Glue one of the whole body pieces on top of the upper and lower bodies. (See Figure 6-23.)

6. Turn the butterfly over.

7. Fold one chenille stick in half and wrap the ends around a pencil to curl them to form the butterfly antennae just as you did for the caterpillar antennae. (See Figure 6-20.)

8. Glue the chenille stick onto the top of the butterfly's head. (See Figure 6-24.)

9. Squirt a bead of glue around the outer edge of the butterfly, leaving an opening at the bottom of the butterfly large enough for your hand to fit through. (See Figure 6-25.)

10. Place the second whole butterfly body piece on top of the glue and press it down firmly.

11. Set the puppet aside for the glue to dry.

Figure 6-23   Butterfly Body

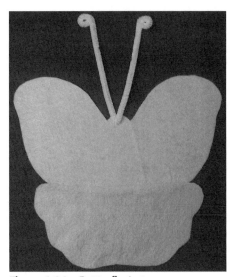

Figure 6-24   Butterfly Antennae

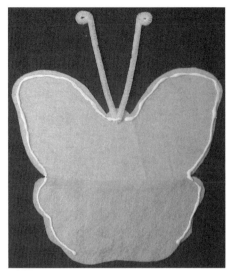

Figure 6-25   Butterfly Gluing

Figure 6-26   Butterfly Felt Puppet

Props

Figure 6-27   Felt Fruit Props

MATERIALS

Green felt scraps for the leaves and stems

One piece of 9-inch by 12-inch red felt for the apple and strawberries

One piece of 9-inch by 12-inch yellow felt for the pears

One piece of 9-inch by 12-inch purple felt for the plums

One piece of 9-inch by 12-inch orange felt for the oranges

Fifteen Craft sticks

DIRECTIONS

1. Photocopy or trace the patterns in the "Puppet Patterns Pantry" on pages 155–158 for the fruit props. Cut out the patterns.
2. Cut fifteen black felt circles for the holes in the fruit.

Apple

1. Cut one apple from red felt.
2. Cut the stem from brown felt.
3. Glue the stem on the apple. (See Figure 6-28.)
4. Glue one black felt circle on the apple.
5. Glue a craft stick on the back of the apple.

Pears

1. Cut two pears from the yellow felt.
2. Cut the stems from the brown felt.
3. Cut the leaves from the green felt.
4. Glue the stems and the leaves on the pears. (See Figure 6-29.)

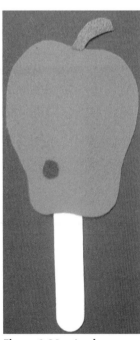

Figure 6-28   Apple

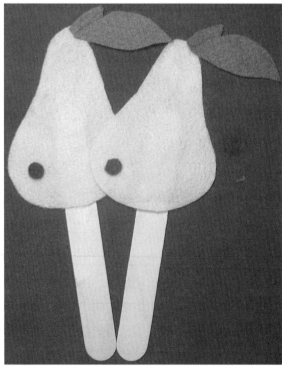

Figure 6-29   Pears

5. Glue a black felt circle on each pear.
6. Glue a craft stick on the back of each pear.

Plums

Figure 6-30   Plums

1. Cut three plums from the purple felt.
2. Cut the leaves from the green felt.
3. Glue the leaves on the plums. (See Figure 6-30.)
4. Glue a black felt circle on each plum.
5. Glue a craft stick on the back of each plum.

Strawberries

1. Cut four strawberries from the red felt.
2. Cut the leaves from the green felt.
3. Glue the leaves on the strawberries. (See Figure 6-31.)
4. Glue a black felt circle on each strawberry.
5. Glue a craft stick on the back of each strawberry.

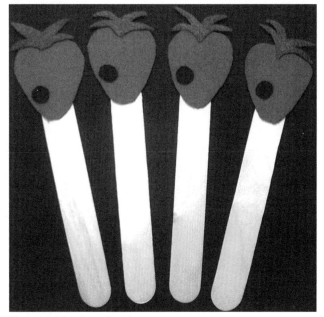

Figure 6-31   Strawberries

Oranges

Figure 6-32   Oranges

1. Cut five oranges from the orange felt.
2. Cut the stems and leaves from the green felt.
3. Glue the stems and leaves on the oranges. (See Figure 6-32.)
4. Glue a black felt circle on each orange.
5. Glue a craft stick on the back of each orange.

III

THE PUPPET
PATTERNS PANTRY

BASIC FELT HAND PUPPET

Photocopy this page at 113%.

Felt Hand Puppet Body

Cut 2

Leave Open

BASIC HAND PUPPET PATTERNS

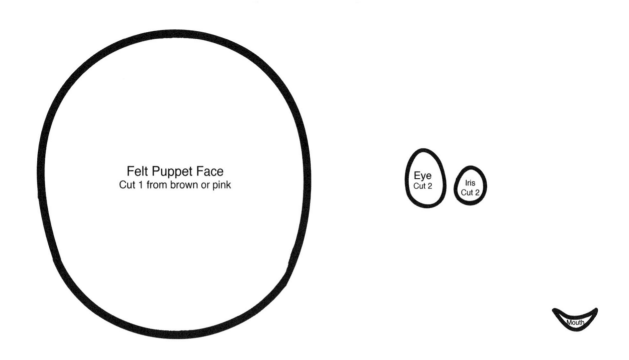

Felt Puppet Face
Cut 1 from brown or pink

Eye
Cut 2

Iris
Cut 2

Mouth

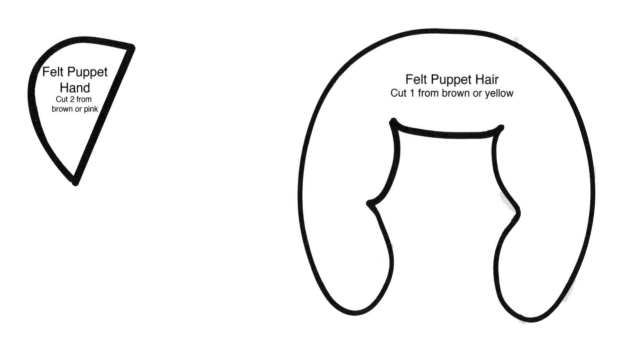

Felt Puppet
Hand
Cut 2 from
brown or pink

Felt Puppet Hair
Cut 1 from brown or yellow

PAPER PLATE PUPPET AND KITTEN

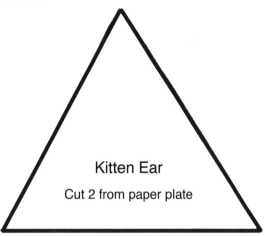

Kitten Ear

Cut 2 from paper plate

Kitten Tongue

Cut 1 of pink felt

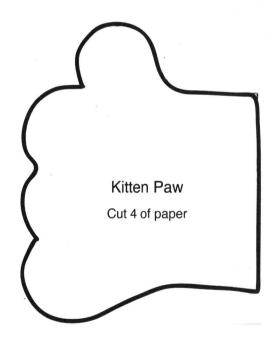

Kitten Paw

Cut 4 of paper

DOG SOCK PUPPET

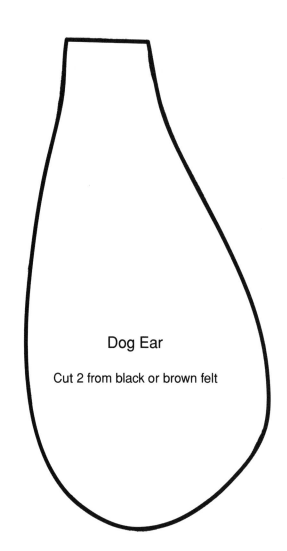

Dog Ear

Cut 2 from black or brown felt

GOAT STICK PUPPET PATTERN

Goat Stick Puppet

Cut 1 from heavy paper

BOY BAND

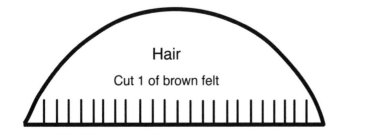

Hair

Cut 1 of brown felt

Nose
Cut 1

OLD MACDONALD PATTERNS

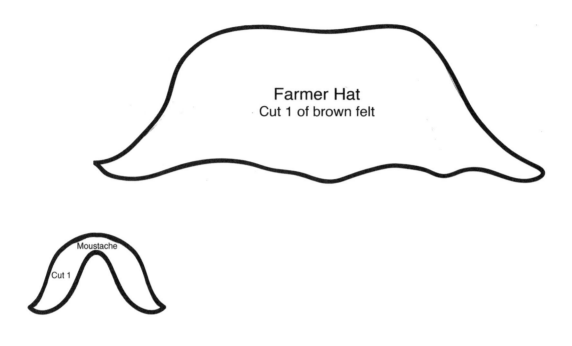

Farmer Hat
Cut 1 of brown felt

Moustache
Cut 1

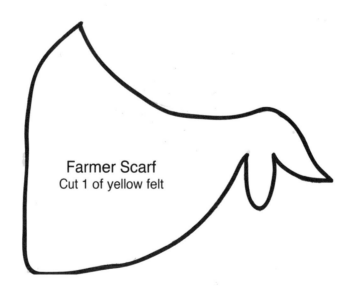

Farmer Scarf
Cut 1 of yellow felt

OLD MACDONALD PATTERNS

Cat
Cut 1 of brown felt

Dog
Cut 1 of brown felt

Dog
Ear
Cut 2

Dog
Tail
Cut 1

OLD MACDONALD PATTERNS

Sheep
Ear
Cut 2

Sheep
Cut 1 of white felt

Cow
Tail
Cut 1

Cow
Cut 1 of brown felt

OLD MACDONALD PATTERNS

OLD LADY PATTERNS

Old Lady Hair Front
Cut 1 of white felt

Fly
Cut 1

Old Lady Hair Back
Cut 1 of white felt

Bird Wing
Cut 1 of felt

Fly
Wing
Cut 1

Spider
Cut 1 of
black felt

Bird
Cut 1 of blue felt

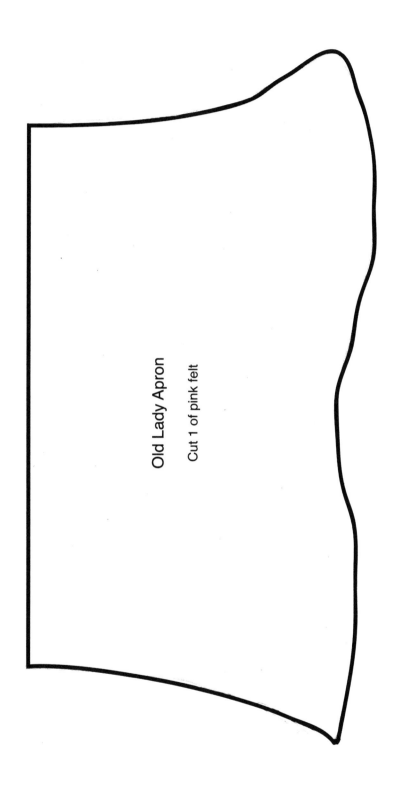

Old Lady Apron

Cut 1 of pink felt

OLD LADY PATTERNS

OLD LADY PATTERNS

Goat
Cut 1 of white felt

FROG PRINCE PATTERNS

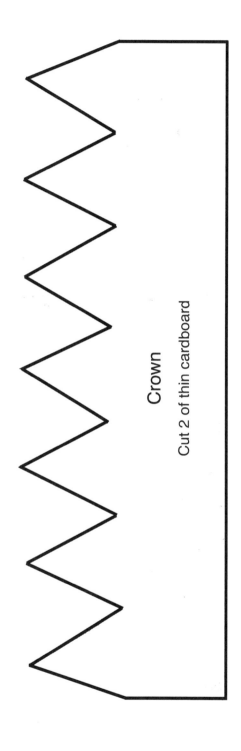

Crown

Cut 2 of thin cardboard

THREE BILLY GOATS PATTERNS

Troll

Cut 1 of heavy paper

THREE BILLY GOATS PATTERNS

Big Billy Goat

Cut 1 of heavy paper

THREE BILLY GOATS PATTERNS

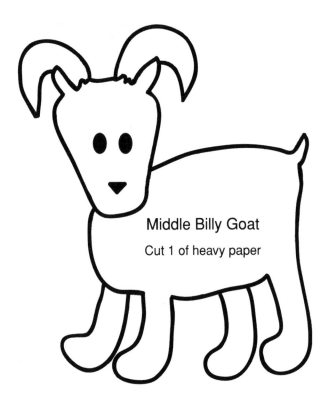

Middle Billy Goat

Cut 1 of heavy paper

Small Billy Goat

Cut 1 of heavy paper

LION AND MOUSE PATTERNS
Photocopy this page at 113%.

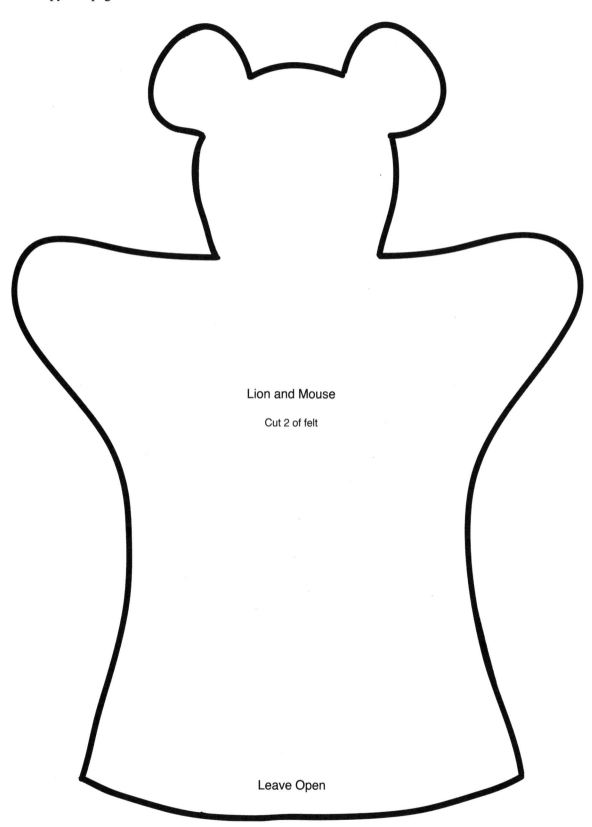

Lion and Mouse

Cut 2 of felt

Leave Open

LION AND MOUSE

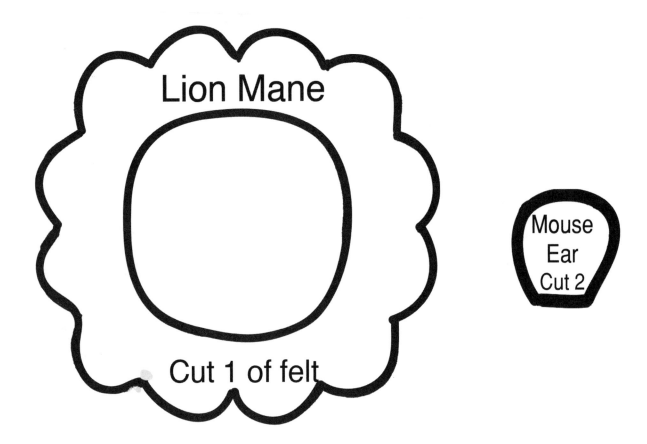

HARE PATTERN

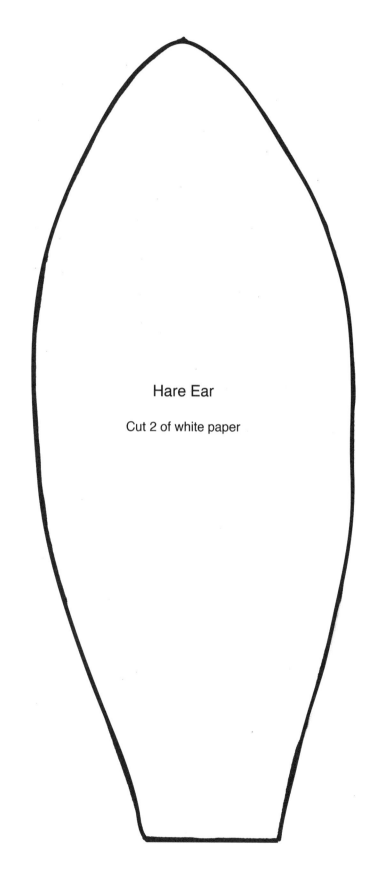

Hare Ear

Cut 2 of white paper

PETER RABBIT PATTERNS

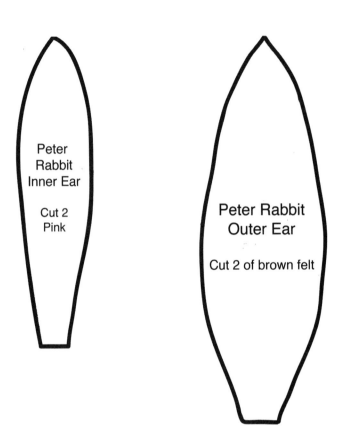

Peter
Rabbit
Inner Ear

Cut 2
Pink

Peter Rabbit
Outer Ear

Cut 2 of brown felt

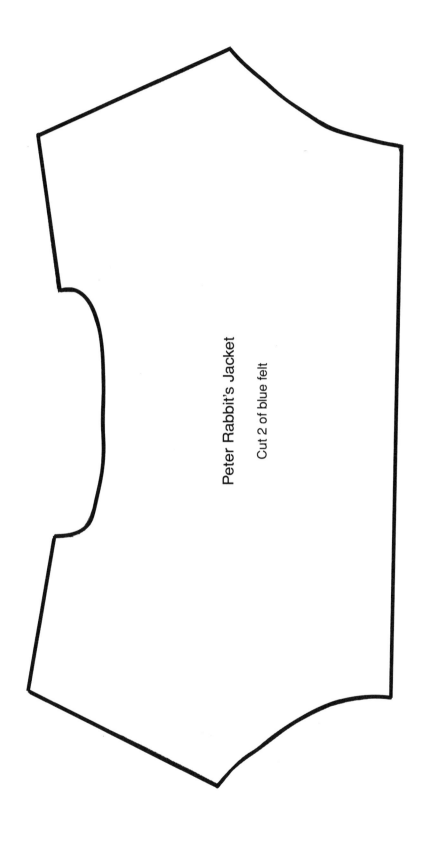

Peter Rabbit's Jacket

Cut 2 of blue felt

PETER RABBIT PATTERNS

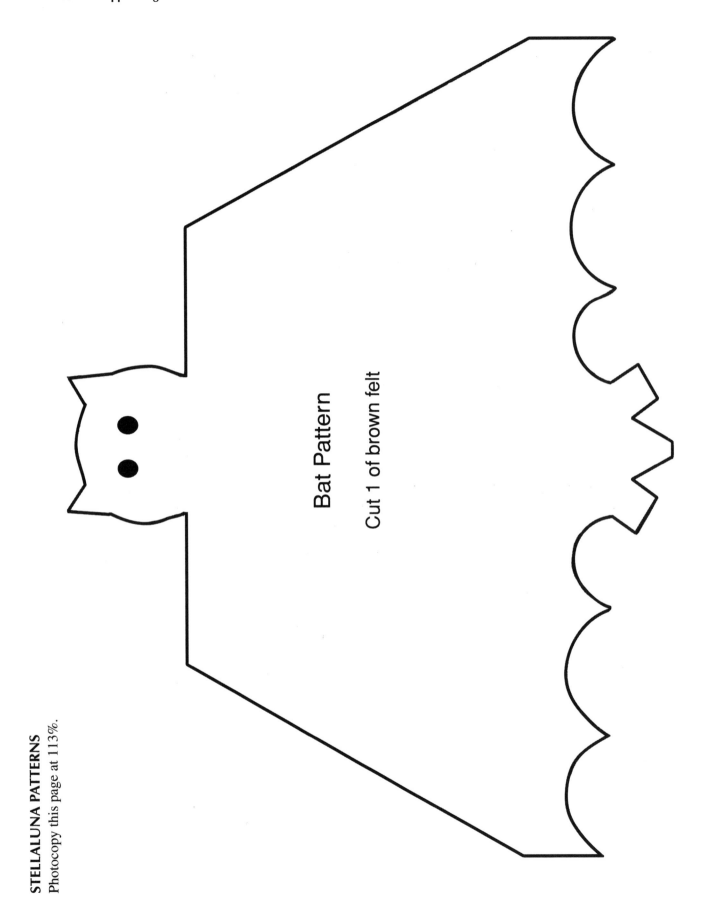

Bat Pattern

Cut 1 of brown felt

STELLALUNA PATTERNS
Photocopy this page at 113%.

SYLVESTER PATTERN

Donkey
Ear
Cut 1

Donkey
Ear
Cut 1

Donkey Head

Cut 2 of brown felt

THE VERY HUNGRY CATERPILLAR PATTERNS
Photocopy this page at 113%.

Butterfly Body

Cut 2 from light blue felt

THE VERY HUNGRY CATERPILLAR PATTERNS

Butterfly Upper Body

Cut 1 from pink felt.

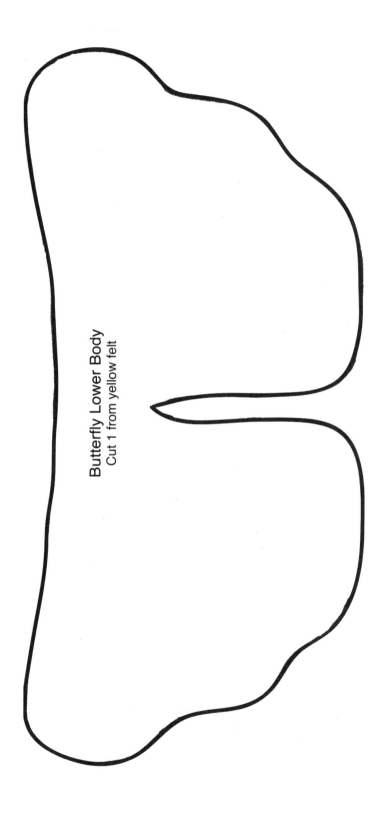

Butterfly Lower Body
Cut 1 from yellow felt

THE VERY HUNGRY CATERPILLAR PATTERNS

THE VERY HUNGRY CATERPILLAR PATTERNS

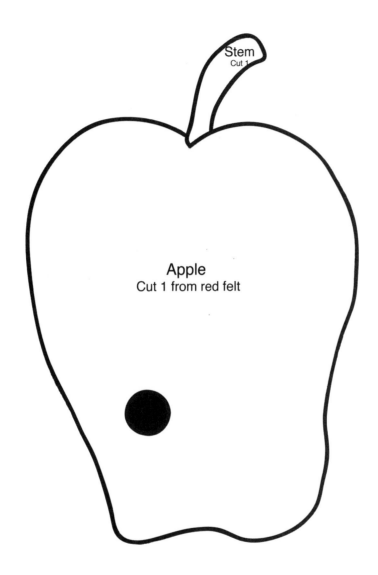

Stem
Cut 1

Apple
Cut 1 from red felt

THE VERY HUNGRY CATERPILLAR PATTERNS

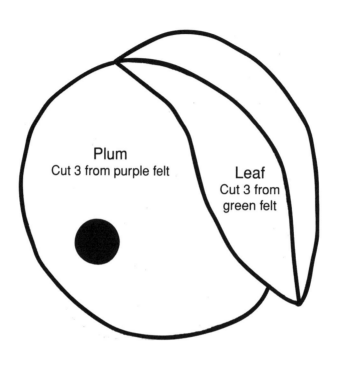

Plum
Cut 3 from purple felt

Leaf
Cut 3 from
green felt

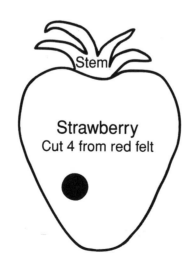

Stem

Strawberry
Cut 4 from red felt

THE VERY HUNGRY CATERPILLAR PATTERNS

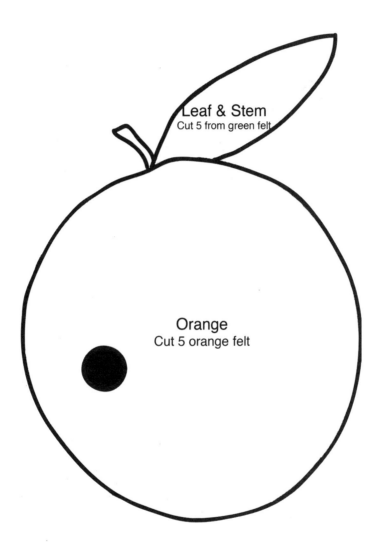

Leaf & Stem
Cut 5 from green felt

Orange
Cut 5 orange felt

THE VERY HUNGRY CATERPILLAR PATTERNS

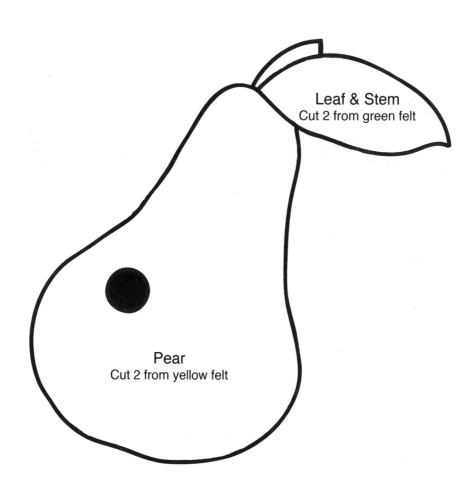

Leaf & Stem
Cut 2 from green felt

Pear
Cut 2 from yellow felt

IV

PUPPET PLANET

A

PUPPET RESOURCES

SOURCES FOR PUPPETS AND ACCESSORIES

Act II Books and Puppets

216 First Street, P.O. Box 1593
Langley, WA 98360
Phone: 360-221-4442
FAX: 360-321-5145
Web site: www.kidsbooks andpuppets.com

Act II has a wealth of resources available for your storybook presentations. It offers Folkmanis puppets, puppet accessories, cuddle toys, dress-up hats, children's books, videos, and audio books. It offers a unique way to store puppets—tree stumps. The tree stumps come in four sizes ranging from 6 inches to 27 inches. They feature holes, branches, and a flat top as options for storing your puppets.

Axtell Expressions: Amazing Professional Puppets and Magic

2889 Bunsen Avenue H
Ventura, CA 93003-1305
Phone: 805-642-7282
FAX: 805-650-2139
Web site: www.axtell.com/

Professional puppets and puppet accessories are available from this Web site. From custom-made puppets to performance tips, there are a variety of resources on the Web site. Information on conferences, puppetry, magic, and ventriloquism are some of the resources found in the links section.

Folkmanis Puppets

1219 Park Avenue
Emeryville, CA 94608
Phone: 800-654-8922
Web site: www.folkmanis.com/index.html

Award-winning Folkmanis puppets are favorites of storytellers. Hand puppets, character puppets, baby Folkmanis puppets, kid glove puppets, and finger puppets can be purchased online. The Web site also has information on where to find a local store that sells Folkmanis puppets. The Web site will direct you to M. S. Creations and Puppets on the Pier to order a catalog of the puppets. Puppets can be purchased online through the Folkmanis Web site. There are also puppets grouped according to environmental theme, therapeutic selections, and storytelling puppets. Storytelling puppets are divided into three categories: animals with moveable mouths, people with moveable mouths, and fantasy theme puppets. Folkmanis also has racks for organizing and displaying puppets.

Highsmith

W5527 State Road 106
P.O. Box 800
Fort Atkinson, WI 53538-0800
Phone: 800-558-2110
FAX: 800-835-2329
Web site: www.highsmith.com

This online store has puppets, puppet play sets, puppet theaters, and puppet storage racks. A site search engine is available for locating specific puppets.

House of Puppetry

7425 Broadacres Road
P.O. Box 29266
Shreveport, LA 71149
Phone: 318-688-6400; 866-865-9828
FAX: 318-688-6403
Web site: www.houseofpuppetry.org

Biblical puppets, character puppets, medical puppets, ethnic puppets, historical figures, and custom-made puppets are manufactured by this nonprofit organization. It also produces programs for puppeteers.

Janis Nelson's Finger Puppets

6700 Welton NE
Albuquerque, NM 87109
Phone: 505-823-2412

Affordable hand-crocheted finger puppets can be bought individually or in story sets. Custom-made and multicultural finger puppets can be ordered.

Let Us Teach Kids

1453 Otoes Place
Jacksonville, FL 32259
Phone: 904-287-2869
FAX: 904-287-2580
Web site: www.letusteachkids.com

If you are looking for sets of people puppets, this is the Web site for you. It offers a wide variety of puppets and resources for puppeteers, including DVDs on puppet manipulation and developing puppet characters.

M. S. Creations

632 East Broadway
Bolivar, MO 65613
Phone/FAX: 888-352-8367
Web site: www.m-s-creations.com

Puppets, books, manipulatives, videos, kites, educational kits, and storytelling props are available from this family-owned company of educators. The puppets are organized into categories including animal, religious, fantasy, finger, and people. This is one source for purchasing Folkmanis puppets.

Manhattan Toy

430 First Avenue N, Suite 500
Minneapolis, MN 55401
Phone: 800-541-1345; 612-337-9600
FAX: 612-341-4457
Web site: www.manhattantoy.com/

Founded in 1979 by Francis Goldwyn (grandson of motion picture studio owner Sam Goldwyn), Manhattan Toy Company pioneered the use of nontraditional fabrics in toy design and introduced delightful new body styles in soft toys. Play takes on new meaning with an inspired collection of puppets that lets a child's imagination shine. Manhattan Toy has many one-of-a-kind hand and finger puppets that provide youngsters with hands-on fun while promoting interactive play and creative expression.

Nancy's Plush Toys and Gifts

807 E. Linden Street
P.O. Box 86
Richland, PA 17087
Phone: 717-866-5487
Web site: www.nancysplushtoys.com

Nancy and her husband started this company about fourteen years ago. It grew from Nancy's hobby of collecting plush toys. In addition to stuffed animals, they offer a variety of puppets organized into these categories: aquatic, cats, dogs, domestic, farm, mythical, people, and wildlife. Puppet theaters are also available.

Playful Puppets

11292 Landy Lane
Great Falls, VA 22066
Phone: 866-501-4931
FAX: 703-433-2411
Web site: www.playfulpuppets.com/

Swallowing puppets, people puppets, monster puppets, hand puppets, and puppets for health professionals are available from this company. The Web site also has information on manipulating swallowing puppets and ideas for using puppets.

Puppet Jungle

Learning Port
831 Jamacha Road
El Cajon, CA 92019
Phone: 888-478-7738
FAX: 888-478-7738
Web site: www.puppetjungle.com

You can search for puppets using the puppet index on the Web site or search by categories. The hand puppets are categorized by prices. There are Folkmanis puppets, biblical characters, book and television characters, puppets for babies, big game trophies, marionettes, monkey mitts, hanging puppets, and finger puppets. This company also has puppet theaters.

Puppet Revelation

17505 Arrowwood Drive
Monument, CO 80132
Phone: 719-302-6074
FAX: 719-302-6075
Web site: www.puppetrevelation.com

This company started in 1997 when Jeanette Lively was home caring for a sick child. She began designing and crafting one-of-a-kind puppets. The company carries specialty puppets such as occupational puppets, human arm puppets, black light puppets, and marionettes. In addition to puppets it has scripts, props, and stages.

The Puppet Store

P&T Puppet Theatre
232 East Acacia Street
Salinas, CA 93901
Phone: 831-754-2411
FAX: 831-597-5100
Web site: www.ptpuppets.com/puppetstore.html

Hand puppets, marionettes, finger puppets, character puppets, fairy tale puppets, and puppet stages can all be purchased from The Puppet Store. Orders can be placed online, by phone, or by fax.

Puppet Universe

14123 93rd Avenue SE
Yelm, WA 98597
Phone: 866-478-7738; 360-400-1236
FAX: 360-400-2186
Web site: www.puppetuniverse.com/

Hand puppets, finger puppets, marionettes, push-up puppets, puppet theaters, and puppet racks are available on this site. There are two search engines. One allows you to search by brand of puppet and the other allows you to search for different kinds of animals.

Puppets on the Pier

Pier 39 Space H-4
San Francisco, CA 94133
Phone: 800-443-4463; 415-781-4435
FAX: 415-379-9544
Web site: www.puppetdream.com

This store features Folkmanis puppets, cartoon and television show puppets, people characters, ventriloquist dolls, marionettes, and puppet theaters. The Web site has a puppets and marionettes glossary. There is a search engine on the Web site that enables you to search for puppets by category.

Puppetville

1221 Berk Avenue
Baltimore, MD 21237-2933
Phone: 410-391-1548
Web site: www.puppetville.com/

Puppetville sells a variety of puppets, puppet clothes, puppet-making kits, and puppet theaters. The Web site offers tips on operating puppets, puppet cleaning instructions, and directions for operating ventriloquist puppets.

Silly Goose Toys

1067 W. Page Avenue
Gilbert, AZ 85233
Phone: 480-813-6307
FAX: 480-813-7850
Web site: www.sillygoosetoys.com/puppet.html

Among the toys on this Web site are a variety of puppet theaters and puppets including hand puppets, finger puppets, and pop-up puppets.

Silly Puppets

266 W. 23rd Street, #437
New York, NY 10011
Phone: 888-211-3826
Web site: www.sillypuppets.com/

The puppets on this Web site are organized by category and come in either 14-inch or 28-inch sizes. Categories include among others animals, babies, fantasy, grandparents, occupations, Christian kids, and sports. There are finger puppets, half-body puppets, real hand puppets, puppet closets, and swallowing puppets.

Sisters in Stitches

2423 Virginia Avenue
Everett, WA 98201
Phone: 425-259-4140; 866-259-4140
FAX: 425-259-3219
Web site: www.sisters-in-stitches.com/

Hand puppets, puppet sets, puppet mitts, and felt board sets are available from this company. Resources for teaching mathematics, science, sign language, and music are also available. Check their online site for the "Old Lady Who Swallowed a Fly" puppet and props.

T & C Creations

905 W 3550 N
Pleasant View, UT 84414
Phone: 801-782-9292
FAX: 801-782-2213
Web site: www.fingerpuppets.net

Finger puppets lovingly handcrafted of acrylic and nylon are sold by this company on its Web site and in stores around the world. The puppets can be bought individually or in sets. The company's classic sets include storybook characters, community helpers, circus animals, and children of the world. It also features holiday sets of finger puppets.

PUPPETRY MUSEUMS

The Ballard Institute and Museum of Puppetry

School of Fine Arts, Depot Campus
University of Connecticut
6 Bourn Place, U-212
Storrs, CT 06269-5212
Phone: 860-486-4605
Web site: www.sp.uconn.edu/~wwwsfa/bimp.html

The museum houses a collection of puppets created and used by the students of Frank Ballard, a professor in the Department of Dramatic Arts. Over the years the museum collection has grown to include different types of puppets from all over the world, some from hundreds of years ago. The Web site includes a gallery of images and a library with articles about puppetry and links to additional resources.

Center for Puppetry Arts

1404 Spring Street NW at 18th
Atlanta, GA 30309-2820
Phone: 404-873-3089
Web site: puppet.org/

The Center for Puppetry Arts has a puppet museum, puppet performances, and educational programs. There is also an online store with books, puppets, DVDs, and figures. The site also has links to a variety of online resources for learning more about puppets.

PUPPETRY ORGANIZATIONS

The Jim Henson Foundation

627 Broadway, 9th floor
New York, NY 10012
Phone: 212-680-1400
FAX: 212-680-1401
Web site: www.hensonfoundation.org/

This foundation established by Jim Henson sponsors innovative puppet theater through grants. The Web site contains a link to the grant guidelines.

Puppet Showplace Theatre

32 Station Street

Brookline, MA 02445

Phone: 617-731-6400

FAX:617-731-0526

Web site: http://www.puppetshowplace.org/

Puppet shows for audiences of all ages, workshops for those interested in using puppetry in education and therapy, and conferences for educators, librarians, and therapists who want to learn how to use puppets are offered by this puppetry resource.

Puppeteers of America

P.O. Box 330

West Liberty, IA 52776

Phone: 888-568-6235

Web site: www.puppeteers.org

This nonprofit organization provides a variety of resources for puppeteers including information on puppet collections, locations of puppet theaters, support for puppetry festivals, an online bulletin board, an audio-video library, and a puppetry store. This organization publishes *The Puppetry Journal* and *The Playboard Newsletter*. Small puppet grants are available for organization members.

The Puppetry Homepage

Web site: www.puppetry.info/puppetry/index.html

This is an amazing collection of puppetry resources with information on organizations, worldwide festivals, theaters, definitions, using puppets, traditions, exhibits, performances, classified ads, scholarships, and workshops.

The Puppetworks Inc.

338 Sixth Avenue (at Fourth Street)

Brooklyn, NY 11215-3403

Phone: 718-965-3391

Web site: www.puppetworks.org/

Located in Brooklyn's Park Slope district, this resident puppet theater features hand-carved wooden marionettes in its performances. The plays presented here come from children's literature, folktales, and fairy tales.

Union Internationale de la Marionnette–USA

1404 Spring Street NW

Atlanta, GA 30309-2820

Phone: 404-873-3089

FAX: 404-873-9907

Web site: unima-usa.org/

This international organization has chapters in forty-three countries around the world and was started in 1929. Jim Henson founded the American branch of this organization in 1966, and it is headquartered at the Center for Puppetry Arts. The organization sponsors conferences, offers scholarships, and publishes a magazine and a newsletter.

B

❦

BIBLIOGRAPHY

Baird, Bil. *The Art of the Puppet*. New York: Macmillan, 1965.

Bauer, Caroline Feller. *Leading Kids to Books through Puppets*. Chicago: American Library Association, 1997.

Buetter, Barbara MacDonald. *Simple Puppets from Everyday Materials*. New York: Sterling, 1996.

Carreiro, Carolyn. *Make Your Own Puppets and Puppet Theaters*. Nashville, TN: Williamson, 2005.

Champlin, Connie. *Storytelling with Puppets*, 2nd ed. Chicago: American Library Association, 1997.

Crepeau, Ingrid M., and M. Ann Richards. *A Show of Hands: Using Puppets with Young Children*. St. Paul, MN: Redleaf, 2003.

Doney, Meryl. *Puppets*. New York: Franklin Watts, 1995.

Engler, Larry, and Carol Fijan. *Making Puppets Come Alive: How to Learn and Teach Hand Puppetry*. Mineola, NY: Dover Publications, 1973.

Faurot, Kimberley K. *Books in Bloom: Creative Patterns & Props That Bring Stories to Life*. Chicago: American Library Association, 2003.

Frey, Yvonne Amar. *One-Person Puppetry Streamlined and Simplified with 38 Folk-Tale Scripts*. Chicago: American Library Association, 2004.

Haines, Ken, and Gill Harvey. *The Usborne Book of Puppets*. Saffron Hill, London: Usborne, 1997.

Henson, Cheryl, and the Muppet Workshop. *The Muppets Make Puppets*. New York: Workman, 1994.

Kennedy, John. 2004. *Puppet Mania!* Cincinnati, OH: North Light Books. (Companion Web site www. puppetkit.com.)

Latshaw, George. *The Complete Book of Puppetry*. Mineola, NY: Dover Publications, 2000.

Lohnes, Marilyn. *Finger Folk: Reading Activities, PK-K*. Fort Atkinson, WI: Alleyside Press, 1999.

Lowe, Joy L., and Kathryn I. Matthew. "Puppets and Prose: Using Puppets and Children's Literature in the Science Classroom." In *Mixing It Up: Integrated, Interdisciplinary, Intriguing Science in the Elementary Classroom* edited by Susan Koba. Arlington, VA: National Science Teachers Association Press, 2003.

Minkel, Walter. *How to Do "The Three Bears" with Two Hands: Performing with Puppets*. Chicago: American Library Association, 2000.

Painter, William M. *Musical Story Hours Using Music with Storytelling and Puppetry*. North Haven, CT: Library Professional Publications, 1989.

———. *Storytelling with Music, Puppets, and Arts for Libraries and Classrooms*. North Haven, CT: Library Professional Publications, 1994.

Ross, Kathy. *Crafts from Your Favorite Nursery Rhymes*. Brookfield, CT: Millbrook Press, 2002.

Ross, Laura. *Hand Puppets: How to Make and Use Them*. Mineola, NY: Dover Publications, 1969.

Rottman, Fran. *Easy-to-Make Puppets and How to Use Them*. Ventura, CA: Gospel Light, 1995.

Sierra, Judy. *Fantastic Theater: Puppets and Plays for Young Performers and Young Audiences*. New York: H. W. Wilson, 1991.

Sierra, Judy, and Robert Kaminski. *Multicultural Folktales: Stories to Tell Young Children*. Phoenix, AZ: Oryx, 1991.

VanSchuyver, Jan. *Storytelling Made Easy with Puppets*. Phoenix, AZ: Oryx, 1993.

C

PUPPETS AND STORIES CHART

Puppet	Title
Bat	*Stellaluna*
Bird	*The Old Lady Who Swallowed a Fly*
Boy	*Jack, Be Nimble*
	Little Tommy Tucker
	Simple Simon
	Wee Willie Winkie
	The Frog Prince
Butterfly	*The Very Hungry Caterpillar*
Cat	*Old MacDonald Had a Farm*
	The Old Lady Who Swallowed a Fly
	Kitten's First Full Moon
Caterpillar	*The Very Hungry Caterpillar*
Cow	*Old MacDonald Had a Farm*
	The Old Lady Who Swallowed a Fly
Dog	*Old MacDonald Had a Farm*
	The Old Lady Who Swallowed a Fly
Fly	*The Old Lady Who Swallowed a Fly*
Girl	*Little Bo-Peep*
	Little Miss Muffet
	Mistress Mary, Quite Contrary
	Polly, Put the Kettle On
	The Frog Prince
Goat	*The Three Billy Goats Gruff*
	Old MacDonald Had a Farm
	The Old Lady Who Swallowed a Fly
Hare	*The Tortoise and the Hare*
	Peter Rabbit
Horse	*Old MacDonald Had a Farm*
	The Old Lady Who Swallowed a Fly
Lady	*The Old Lady Who Swallowed a Fly*
Lion	*The Lion and the Mouse*
Man	*Old MacDonald Had a Farm*

Puppet	Title
Mouse	*The Lion and the Mouse*
Snake	*Verdi*
Tortoise	*The Tortoise and the Hare*
Troll	*The Three Billy Goats Gruff*

Index

About the Authors

Kathryn I. Matthew is a former classroom teacher and is an associate professor at the University of Houston–Clear Lake. She received graduate and undergraduate degrees from the University of New Orleans. She received an Ed.D. in Curriculum and Instruction with an emphasis on technology and reading from the University of Houston. Kathryn and Joy co-authored the *Neal-Schuman Guide to Recommended Children's Books and Media for Use with Every Elementary Subject* and the *Neal-Schuman Guide to Celebrations and Holidays Around the World*. Kathryn also wrote *Developing Better Readers and Writers Using Caldecott Books* published by Neal-Schuman. She lives in Sugar Land, Texas, with her husband, Chip.

Joy L. Lowe is a former school and public librarian, and she taught library science at Louisiana Tech University for thirty years. She received graduate and undergraduate degrees from Centenary College of Louisiana, Louisiana Tech University, and Louisiana State University. She received a Ph.D. in Library and Information Science from the University of North Texas. Kathryn and Joy co-authored the *Neal-Schuman Guide to Recommended Children's Books and Media for Use with Every Elementary Subject* and the *Neal-Schuman Guide to Celebrations and Holidays Around the World*. Joy lives in Ruston, Louisiana, with her husband, Perry.